SCIENCE FICTION

From groundbreaking novels of ideas to blockbusters on the cinema screen, science fiction is all around us. This volume offers a clear and critically engaged account of the SF phenomenon, from its earliest origins to the present.

Adam Roberts examines the history of science fiction and the critical debate which surrounds this, providing beginners with a springboard for further study, but also challenging more advanced students with original interpretations of key SF texts. These range from Ursula Le Guin's 1969 feminist SF novel *The Left Hand of Darkness*, to Barry Sonnenfeld's 1997 blockbuster film *Men in Black*. Roberts introduces essential critical terminology, looking in detail at concepts of alien, cyborg, spaceship and robot, and tackling issues such as gender, race, technology and science fiction/science fact.

This guided tour through science fiction constitutes an inspired introduction to the field and a brilliant new perspective on a major cultural force.

Adam Roberts is Reader in English at Royal Holloway, University of London. His SF novel *Salt* (Gollancz 2000) was shortlisted for the Arthur C. Clarke award. His second novel *On* (Gollancz 2001) is now available.

THE NEW CRITICAL IDIOM

SERIES EDITOR: JOHN DRAKAKIS, UNIVERSITY OF STIRLING

The New Critical Idiom is an invaluable series of introductory guides to today's critical terminology. Each book:

- provides a handy, explanatory guide to the use (and abuse) of the term
- offers an original and distinctive overview by a leading literary and cultural critic
- relates the term to the larger field of cultural representation

With a strong emphasis on clarity, lively debate and the widest possible breadth of examples, *The New Critical Idiom* is an indispensable approach to key topics in literary studies.

SCIENCE FICTION

Adam Roberts

Routledge
Taylor & Francis Group

LONDON AND NEW YORK

First published 2000
by Routledge
11 New Fetter Lane, London EC4P 4EE

Simultaneously published in the USA and Canada
by Routledge
29 West 35th Street, New York, NY 10001

Reprinted 2002 , 2003 (twice)

Routledge is an imprint of the Taylor & Francis Group

© 2000 Adam Roberts

Typeset in Garamond by Taylor & Francis Books Ltd
Printed and bound in Great Britain by TJ International Ltd,
Padstow, Cornwall

British Library Cataloguing in Publication Data
A catalogue record for this book is available from the British Library

Library of Congress Cataloging-in-Publication Data
Roberts, Adam (Adam Charles)
    Science fiction/Adam Roberts.
    p.cm.
    Includes bibliographical references and index.
    1. Science fiction—History and criticism. I. Title.
    P96.S34 R58   1999
    809.3'8762–dc21   99-087223

ISBN 0–415–19204–8 (hbk)
ISBN 0–415–19205–6 (pbk)

CONTENTS

SERIES EDITOR'S PREFACE

The New Critical Idiom is a series of introductory books which seeks to extend the lexicon of literary terms, in order to address the radical changes which have taken place in the study of literature during the last decades of the twentieth century. The aim is to provide clear, well-illustrated accounts of the full range of terminology currently in use, and to evolve histories of its changing usage.

The current state of the discipline of literary studies is one where there is considerable debate concerning basic questions of terminology. This involves, among other things, the boundaries which distinguish the literary from the non-literary; the position of literature within the larger sphere of culture; the relationship between literatures of different cultures; and questions concerning the relation of literary to other cultural forms within the context of interdisciplinary studies.

It is clear that the field of literary criticism and theory is a dynamic and heterogeneous one. The present need is for individual volumes on terms which combine clarity of exposition with an adventurousness of perspective and a breadth of application. Each volume will contain as part of its apparatus some indication of the direction in which the definition of particular terms is likely to move, as well as expanding the disciplinary boundaries within which some of these terms have been traditionally contained. This will involve some re-situation of terms within the larger field of cultural representation, and will introduce examples from the area of film and the modern media, in addition to examples from a variety of literary texts.

ACKNOWLEDGEMENTS

I would like to thank the following people for input, advice, help and support. John Drakakis has done more than is usually required of a series editor, and his advice has made this a much better book than it would otherwise have been. Liz Brown's support has been superb and invaluable. Bob Eaglestone read the entire manuscript and made many helpful suggestions. I would also like to thank Geraldine Glennon, Roger Luckhurst, Abraham Kawa, Julie Roberts, Talia Rogers, Sarah Kennedy and Sara Salih. Discussion and interaction with the students on the course *Science Fiction and Fantasy* at Royal Holloway, University of London for the years 1997–8 and 1999–2000 has taught me a great deal about SF.

1

DEFINING SCIENCE FICTION

ONE DEFINITION

The term 'science fiction' resists easy definition. This is curious, because most people have a sense of what science fiction is. Any bookstore will have a section devoted to SF: shelves of mostly brightly-coloured paperback volumes, illustrated on their covers with photorealist paintings of intricate spaceships perhaps, or of men and women in futuristic cities or bizarre alien landscapes. Most of these novels are narratives that elaborate some imaginative or fantastic premise, perhaps involving a postulated future society, encounters with creatures from another world, travel between planets or in time. In other words, science fiction as a genre or division of literature distinguishes its fictional worlds to one degree or another from the world in which we actually live: a fiction of the imagination rather than observed reality, a fantastic literature.

But when it comes down to specifying in what way SF is distinctive, and in what ways it is different from other imaginative and fantastic literatures, there is disagreement. All of the many definitions offered by critics have been contradicted or modified by other critics, and it is always possible to point to texts consensually called SF that fall outside the usual definitions. It is, perhaps, for this reason that some critics try to content themselves with definitions of the mode that are mere tautologies, as if 'we' all know what it is and elaboration is superfluous. Edward James suggests that 'SF is what is marketed as SF' (although he concedes that, as a definition, this is 'a beginning, nothing more') (James 1994: 3). Damon Knight says that 'science fiction is what we point to when we say it'; and Norman Spinraid argues that 'science fiction is anything published as science fiction' (quoted in Clute and Nicholls 1993: 314). There is a kind of weariness in this sort of circular reasoning, underlain by a sense that the whole business of definition is nothing more than a marketing exercise. Lance Parkin suggests that 'SF is a notoriously difficult term to define, but when it comes down to it, a book appears on the SF shelves if the publisher thinks they will maximize their sales by labelling it as such' (Parkin 1999: 4). This mistrust of definition has interesting implications for the self-image of SF as a genre, although it doesn't get us very far as a starting point.

The *Oxford English Dictionary* defines science fiction as 'imaginative fiction based on postulated scientific discoveries or spectacular environmental changes, frequently set in the future or on other planets and involving space or time travel', adding that the term did not come into common usage until the 1920s. The terms of this basic dictionary definition are instructive: 'imaginative fiction' differentiates SF from 'realist' fiction, in which there is some attempt at a literary verisimilitude that reproduces the experience of living in the world we recognise as ours. Where the realist writer needs to focus on accuracy, the SF author can use her imagination to invent things not found in our world. These points of difference, the 'scientific discoveries' or 'environmental changes' of the dictionary definition, may be such things as 'space or time travel' but they could be many other premises not listed by the OED, to do with robots, computers, alternative histories and the like. This makes SF a literature of ideas predicated on some substantive difference or differences between the world described and the world in which readers actually live.

The date is important too. Novels and stories written in what is generally known as science fiction were certainly produced before the 1920s – for example, in the late nineteenth century by writers such as H G Wells and Jules Verne. Some critics assert that the first SF story comes from even earlier than that. Mary Shelley's *Frankenstein* (1818), the story of a strange new form of life created by science, has been put forward as the first SF text by several critics (Aldiss 1973). There are also critics who have argued for a more ancient provenance even than that, to Thomas More's *Utopia* (1516) or the adventures of Baron Munchausen. Chapter 2 of the present study explores these contested versions of the history of SF. But none of these books just mentioned belonged to a recognised *genre* – a specific type or species of literature – called Science Fiction. In their own day they were called Gothic tales, *contes fantastiques* ('fantastic stories'), scientific romances and other various designations. In other words, they were specific and sometimes one-off examples of imaginative fiction. It was not until the 1920s that these sorts of writing became identified as belonging to a family of literature, Science Fiction.

But whilst SF is imaginative fiction, it does not follow that all imaginative fiction can be usefully categorised as SF. Stories in which the protagonists travel from Earth to colonies on Mars by rocket ship are usually taken to be science fiction because no such colonies, and no such available mode of transport, are available to us today. But fairytales, surreal fictions (such as Andre Breton's *Nadja*, 1928), or magic realism (like Salman Rushdie's *Midnight's Children*, 1981) all involve substantive differences between the world of the text and the world the readership actually lives in, and they are not categorised as science fiction. For example, there is a novel by Ian Watson called *The Jonah Kit* (1975), which involves a new technology that maps the brainwave patterns of a human onto the mind of a whale. This human consciousness then inhabits the whale. We might compare this tale with Franz Kafka's short novel *Metamorphosis* (1915), in which the protagonist wakes up one morning to find himself transformed into the shape of a giant insect. Watson's novel is classified as SF, where Kafka's is not. Why should this be? Both are imaginative fictions based on the premise of a radical change; neither are concerned with space or time travel, or are set on other planets. What makes them different?

There could be two answers to this question. The first would assert that science fiction is a much broader category than is usually admitted, and should be used to describe a wide range of 'fantasy' literatures; according to this argument, Kafka's *Metamorphosis* is indeed a science-fiction tale, even if it is not usually categorised as such. The second argument would deny this, and stress the differences of approach of the two writers. Kafka never explains how his hero turns into a bug: the metamorphosis is literally inexplicable, a physical impossibility. Indeed, Kafka isn't interested in the change as such, which is why he does not feel any need to explain how it has come about. He is interested in the alienation his character subsequently suffers, the reactions of his family to his new monstrosity. In other words the transformation of man into bug is only a premise, a symbolic facilitator for the subsequent narrative and not a focus for narrative explication in itself. Watson's metamorphosis of man into whale, on the other hand, is placed in a context of scientific research and is given a particular rationalisation, an explanation for how it has come about. This change does not 'just happen', it is *made* to happen via a machine that reads brainwave patterns and reproduces them in another brain. This is not to say, quite, that Watson's metamorphosis is 'scientific' where Kafka's is, we might say, 'arbitrary' or 'magical'. Science today could not effect the sort of change upon which Watson's book is premised, and it is a moot question whether it ever will be able to.

It is equally impossible, in strict scientific terms, to manipulate DNA to create dinosaurs in the ways required by Michael Crichton's book *Jurassic Park* (1993), or to design spaceships that can travel between the stars like *Star Trek*'s USS *Enterprise*. But it is part of the logic of SF, and not of other forms of fiction, that these changes be made plausible within the structure of the text. This means that the premise of an SF novel requires material, physical rationalisation, rather than a supernatural or arbitrary one. This grounding of SF in the material rather than the supernatural becomes one of its key features. Sometimes this materialism is rooted in a 'scientific' outlook – science is, after all, one of the dominant materialist discourses of the present day. But sometimes the materialism is not, strictly speaking, scientific. Stephen Baxter's *Titan* (1998) is a novel about a journey of space exploration to Jupiter. Everything that happens in that novel adheres strictly to scientific laws as Baxter understands them – his characters even re-use the tried-and-tested technology of the Saturn V Moon programme from the 1970s. Kim Stanley Robinson's *Red Mars* (1992) also begins with a journey of exploration to another planet, again carefully imagined so as not to violate the constraints of current science and technology. Later in Robinson's novel a technique is discovered for hugely extending human lifespan. This is certainly *not* within the discourse of current science, and may well be impossible, but the plot development is integrated into the pseudo-scientific idiom of the book. Instead of just asserting without explaining, as a magic-realist or surrealist writer might, that his characters can now postpone growing old for hundreds of years, Robinson introduces a material device, a gene-resplicing bath, to explain and make plausible this idea.

To give another example of the contrast between SF and other fiction: John Updike's magic-realist novel *Brazil* (1994) tells the story of two lovers, a black boy and a white girl. In the course of the novel, the skin colours of these two figures change such that by the end of the book the boy is white and the girl black. This

change is not rationalised in terms of the fictional world the characters inhabit, which is in all other respects a closely observed
representation of contemporary South America; it is exactly the
kind of unexplained literary device we associate with magic realism. On the other hand there is a novel by John Kessel called
Good News From Outer Space (1995) set in the near-future USA,
one part of which is concerned with a new drug which alters skin
pigmentation. Characters in the novel plan to release this drug in
the American water supply as a terrorist gesture to undermine
the ingrained racism of their society. Once again, we are tempted
to call Kessel's book science fiction and Updike's not. Although
both books are making points about the arbitrariness of racial
definition by positing an interchangeability of skin colour, Kessel
provides a specific mechanism for this change and Updike does
not. Kessel's imaginary drug is not scientific – it does not and
probably could not actually exist – but it is a material device and
within the realm of the discourse it inhabits it is a plausible facilitator. Kessel's science fiction depends upon a certain premise,
and that premise is symbolic of change. In other words, the drug
is a symbol in terms of the text, but it is a concrete and material
symbol that is integrated into a certain discourse of scientific possibility. Updike's text dispenses with the need for such a symbol.

It seems that this 'point of difference', the thing or things that
differentiate the world portrayed in science fiction from the world
we recognise around us, is the crucial separator between SF and
other forms of imaginative or fantastic literature. The critic
Darko Suvin has usefully coined the term 'novum', the Latin for
'new' or 'new thing', to refer to this 'point of difference' (the plural is 'nova'). An SF text may be based on one novum, such as the
device that enables H G Wells's hero to travel through time in
The Time Machine (1895). More usually it will be predicated on a
number of interrelated nova, such as the varieties of futuristic
technology found aboard the starship *Enterprise* in *Star Trek*, from
faster-than-light travel to matter-transportation machines. This

'novum' must not be supernatural, but need not necessarily be a piece of technology. The central 'novum' of Ursula Le Guin's *The Left Hand of Darkness* (1969), for instance, is a different model of gender, although there are other, more technological 'nova' in that book, including interstellar transport and a hyperspace walkie-talkie called an 'ansible'. Unlike such premises as the human inexplicably metamorphosed into an insect in Kafka's story, these nova are grounded in a discourse of possibility, which is usually science or technology, and which renders the difference a *material* rather than just a conceptual or imaginative one. The emphasis is on difference, and the systematic working out of the consequences of a difference or differences, of a novum or nova, becomes the strength of the mode.

THREE DEFINITIONS

There have been a great many attempts to define science fiction in more exact terms than these. Once we accept that the particularities of the 'novum' distinguish SF from other forms of imaginative literature, the urge is to elaborate the sorts of literary context in which these nova are elaborated – to flesh out, in other words, the broader features of the SF text beyond its notional, material point of difference with our familiar world.

It is worth detailing three definitions of SF that have had a great deal of influence on the study of the subject, from three influential critics: Darko Suvin, Robert Scholes and Damien Broderick. First there is respected elder statesman of SF criticism, Darko Suvin, who in 1979 defined SF as:

> a literary genre whose necessary and sufficient conditions are the presence and interaction of estrangement and cognition, and whose main formal device is an imaginative framework alternative to the author's empirical environment.
>
> (Suvin 1979: 8–9)

'Cognition', with its rational, logical implications, refers to that aspect of SF that prompts us to try and understand, to comprehend the alien landscape of a given SF book, film or story. 'Estrangement' is a term from Brecht, more usually rendered in English-language criticism as 'alienation'; and in this context it refers to that element of SF that we recognise as different, that 'estranges' us from the familiar and everyday. If the SF text were entirely concerned with 'estrangement' then we would not be able to understand it; if it were entirely to do with 'cognition' then it would be scientific or documentary rather than science fiction. According to Suvin, both features need to be present; and it is this co-presence that allows SF both relevance to our world *and* the position to challenge the ordinary, the taken-for-granted. The main 'formal device' of Suvin's version of SF is the novum.

Suvin goes on to insist that this 'alternative' world of SF, determined by 'estrangement' and 'cognition', must be *possible*, by which he means it must reflect the constraints of science. This is how he distinguishes SF from the looser category of 'fantasy'. Indeed, it seems from reading Suvin that, for him, 'cognitive' is almost a synonym for 'scientific'; that his phrase 'cognitive estrangement' is just another way of restating the phrase that is to be defined, 'science fiction'. One of the strengths of Suvin's definition is that it seems to embody a certain common-sense tautology, that science fiction is scientific fictionalising. But, as we have seen, science is just as frequently represented in the SF novel by pseudo-science, by some device outside the boundaries of science that is none the less rationalised in the *style* of scientific discourse. We might want to define 'science' as a body of observations and derived laws established by experiment in the real world; but, according to this definition, several of the frequently deployed 'nova' of SF are things that 'science' has specifically ruled out of court as literally impossible. The most obvious example of this is faster-than-light travel, a staple of a great many SF tales but something that scientists assure us can never happen.

Rather than abandon the rationale of science, though, SF stories that involve 'faster-than-light' travel slip into the idiom of 'pseudo-science', providing rationalisations of these impossible activities in terms that *sound like* scientific discourse.

For Suvin, the important thing about the 'science' part of 'science fiction' is that it is a discourse built on certain logical principles that avoids self-contradiction; that it is *rational* rather than emotional or instinctual. Scientists sometimes like to assert that they deal in 'facts' and 'truth', where fiction deals in 'imagination' and is a form of lying. But it is more accurate to describe science as a discipline based on falsifiability, a discourse in which hypotheses are tested by experiment. Accordingly, whilst a scientific premise may be proved false, it cannot be proved true. In science fiction it is not that the use of science gives the texts a particular, privileged access to truth. Often the reverse is true. Gwyneth Jones points out that Larry Niven's *Ringworld* (1970), 'one of the great, classic "engineering feat" SF novels, reached print in the first instance with terrible mistakes in its science' (Jones 1999: 16). Niven revised the novel for subsequent publication after fans pointed out a number of scientific impossibilities, but Jones makes the point that 'the challenge, which had to be met, was not to Niven's scientific accuracy, but to his appearance of command over the *language* of science'. Many early SF novels followed the scientific thinking of the day and imagined canals on Mars, oceans on Venus. The fact that more recent scientific experiment has concluded that there are no such canals or oceans does not invalidate these novels, because the point about the science in SF is not 'truth' but the entry into a particular, material and often rational discourse. To quote Jones again:

> 'Science' in Science Fiction has always had a tacit meaning other than that commonly accepted. It had nothing in particular to say about the subject matter, which may be just about anything so long as the formal conventions of future dress are

> observed. It means only, finally, that whatever phenomenon or speculation is treated in the fiction, there is a claim that it is going to be studied to some extent scientifically – that is objectively, rigorously; in a controlled environment. The business of the writer is to set up the equipment in a laboratory of the mind such that the 'what if' in question is at once isolated and provided with the exact nutrients it needs.
>
> (Jones 1999: 4)

Jones sees SF as a form of thought experiment, an elaborate 'what if?' game where the consequences of some or other nova are worked through. In other words, it is not the 'truth' of science that is important to SF; it is the scientific method, the logical working through of a particular premise. This is precisely what Suvin asserts: 'SF is distinguished by the narrative dominance or hegemony of a fictional "novum"...validated by cognitive logic' (Suvin 1979: 63). By this he means that the implications of the 'novum' dominate, or create a 'hegemony' (a term from Marxist theory to describe the maintenance of power by indirect and pervasive means rather than by direct force) throughout the text. 'Cognitive Logic' becomes for Suvin a crucial formal convention of SF.

If Suvin takes his starting point from the 'science' part of 'science fiction', another highly influential critic has concentrated more on the literary features of SF texts. Robert Scholes, in his book *Structural Fabulation*, has stressed the metaphorical strain of SF. He defines 'fabulation' as any 'fiction that offers us a world clearly and radically discontinuous from the one we know, yet returns to confront that known world in some cognitive way' (Scholes 1975: 2). This point of 'discontinuity' with the known world is the Suvinian novum, but Scholes has a different emphasis. He wants to acknowledge that SF is interested in things being different from the world we actually inhabit, but does not want to concede that this makes SF merely escapist or irrelevant.

According to Scholes, SF is both different and the same, both 'discontinuous' from our world and also 'confronting' that world 'in some cognitive way'. Scholes notes that 'fabulation' is a category including any and all fantastic or imaginative literature, including non-SF writers like Borges, Thomas Pynchon and Herman Hesse, to mention three of Scholes's own examples. Accordingly, Scholes adds 'structural' to his 'fabulation' definition in order to pin things down more tightly. As with Suvin, there's a certain re-duplication here. 'Fabulation' seems synonymous with 'fiction' in pretty much the same way that 'structural' is with science: we could abbreviate both 'science fiction' and 'structural fabulation' to SF if we wanted to. In fact, Scholes's point is a little more subtle than that. For him, SF is permeated by 'an awareness of the universe as a system of systems, a structure of structures'. Whilst he concedes that, for SF, 'the insights of the past century of science are accepted as fictional points of departure', he is none the less adamant that SF is more than just a 'scientific' version of fabulation. 'Structural fabulation is neither scientific in its methods, nor a substitute for actual science. It is a fictional exploration of human situations made perceptible by the implications of recent science.' Damien Broderick has praised Scholes as 'one of the first American scholars to recover SF from the trash can and announce a place for it in the academy' (Broderick 1995: 29); and one of the reasons Scholes thinks so highly of SF is because of the possibilities it opens up as a distinctive, twentieth-century 'scientific' mode of literature. More particularly, 'science', which is an observational method, is only the starting point for Scholes's SF. He is more interested in the fictionalisation of the premise, and accordingly his emphasis is rather different from Suvin's.

This 'scientific' – cognitive, rational, categorical – approach to the issues of defining the genre has the upper hand in much critical discussion of SF. Damien Broderick, an SF author as well as being a theoretically-engaged critic, concludes his analysis of the contemporary SF scene with the following definition of what SF is now:

> Sf is that species of storytelling native to a culture undergoing the epistemic changes implicated in the rise and supercession of technical–industrial modes of production, distribution, consumption and disposal. It is marked by (i) metaphoric strategies and metonymic tactics, (ii) the foregrounding of icons and interpretative schemata from a collectively constituted generic 'mega-text' and the concomitant de-emphasis of 'fine writing' and characterisation, and (iii) certain priorities more often found in scientific and postmodern texts than in literary models: specifically, attention to the object in preference to the subject.
>
> (Broderick 1995: 155)

The sheer complexity of this definition enacts the pseudo-scientific discourse that is also at the heart of much SF. By 'metaphoric strategies and metonymic tactics' Broderick means that, whilst the overall drift of any given SF text will be to represent the world metaphorically, such that the whole SF-imagined world encodes a part of the real world, the actual elements in the novel itself will not be metaphorical but *metonymic*. The difference is that in metaphor a whole things stands in for another thing: in the phrase 'the ship of state', a notional ship is figuratively representing the state. In metonymy, a part of a thing stands in for the whole thing, as when a priest refers to his congregation as 'ninety souls' rather than 'ninety people'. Structuralist critic Roman Jakobson has argued that what he called the 'vertical' axis of metaphor and the 'horizontal' axis of metonymy between them describe the way language signifies. Broderick explains that 'the strategy of estrangement uses one thing as a figure or stand-in for another' as metaphor does, and gives the example of '30 Heads of State'. This, he suggests, is 'the mechanism of poetry and allegory'. On the other hand, he argues that 'usually prose fictions employ a strategy of *metonymy*...part standing for whole, 30 Heads of Cattle' (Broderick 1995: 34).

To put this another way, we might say the 'novum' of SF is a part of the imagined world that stands in for the process of a whole environment; whereas the *whole SF text* operates metaphorically. Many of these devices, as Broderick mentions, derive from a corpus of accepted 'nova', such as starships, time-machines, robots and the like. Each of these connects with a particular 'estranged' version of our reality. A film such as *Blade Runner* (1982), for instance, contains androids, artificial humans of great beauty and strength but whose existence is hollow because their four-year lifespan does not give them the time to develop full humanity. They are good-looking but shallow, and as nova they symbolically connect with the overall logic of the film, which is often taken as a 'postmodern' artefact more concerned with style than substance, with surface rather than depth. But the film as a whole, we might argue, stands as a metaphor for the alienated existence of contemporary life. (I should add that this particular example is not taken from Broderick's work.) Broderick sees SF as an open-ended cultural phenomenon, which is particularly good at reflecting times of great cultural and technological change, of which our present age is a good example.

Broderick develops and deepens the Suvinian sense of 'cognitive estrangement' and Scholes's 'structural fabulation'; but he also brings in aspects not dwelt upon by either of those critics. In particular, he is very aware of SF as a *popular* genre, one that shares many features with other 'pulp' fictions and popular modes: what he calls a 'de-emphasis on fine writing' and the use of a range of accepted or even worn-out conventional 'icons' – the mad scientist, say; or the robot yearning for humanity. Lurking behind this is a sense that SF is popular because it is populist, that it panders to the lowest common denominator, that it is an adolescent mode of writing, that it is not 'serious' or 'high art'.

Broderick's perspective here is part of a larger critical unease about SF as a genre, a sense that it does not provide readers with many of the things that serious literature does – with, for instance, beautiful or experimental writing styles, detailed and subtle analyses of character or psychological analyses. Of course it is possible to think of SF texts that do these things, but most do not. Instead of style, SF texts often concentrate on concept, subject and narrative. Instead of the abstract, SF texts prefer the concrete, so, rather than meditate upon 'alienness', a SF novel is more likely to present us with an actual, concretely realised alien, with blue skin and bug eyes. According to SF author and critic Gwyneth Jones, SF avoids the trappings of mainstream fiction so as not to distract its readership from the conceptual experiment it represents; fine writing is 'de-emphasised' in order to allow content and concept to come more obviously to the fore. 'A typical science fiction novel has little space for deep and studied characterisation,' argues Jones, 'not because writers lack the skill (although they may) but because in the final analysis the characters are not people, they are pieces of equipment...the same reductive effect is at work on the plot, where naked, artless ur-scenarios of quest, death and desire are openly displayed' (Jones 1999: 5). This is a version of Broderick's suggestion that SF is more interested in 'object' than subject.

It is hard to deny that many SF texts are limited and narrow if judged by the aesthetic criteria sometimes applied to other literatures; that their characterisation often is thin, their style dull and unadventurous, their plots hackneyed. Moreover, the nova that differentiate the SF world from the recognisable world of realist fiction are more often than not drawn from a fairly narrow range of stock themes and situations. In fact it is possible to categorise the major tropes of SF in half a dozen categories. Books that take any of the following subjects, themes, trappings or props are liable to be thought of as science fiction:

- Spaceships, interplanetary or interstellar travel;
- Aliens and the encounter with aliens;
- Mechanical robots, genetic engineering, biological robots ('androids');
- Computers, advanced technology, virtual reality;
- Time travel;
- Alternative history;
- Futuristic utopias and dystopias.

A body of literature built on so narrow a base of premises runs the risk of becoming repetitive and crude in practice, and Broderick sometimes gives the impression of picking only a few exceptional texts from a morass of formulaic and mass-market examples. He talks of 'the poverty of mass-market SF' being 'visible even in the new work of attested and once-fresh writers' of the calibre of Asimov.

There can be a wearying sense of deja vu in reading a new SF novel. Broderick himself quotes the blurbs from recent SF publishers' catalogues to illustrate that SF nova have in large part lost all newness because of their endless circulation and recirculation:

CYBERSTEALTH, S. N. Lewitt – The cyberstealth pilots are the best of the breed. But Cargo, the best of the best, needs more than expert flying to seek and destroy a traitor.

REVENGE OF THE VALKYRIE, Thorarinn Gunnarsson – Here is the blazing epic sequel to *Song of the Dwarves*.

GUARDIANS OF THE THREE VOL II. KEEPER OF THE CITY, Bill Fawcett – This is a magnificent epic of adventure, romance and wizardry set in the unique world of the catlike mrem.

BROTHER TO DEMONS, BROTHER TO GODS, Jack Williamson – From the test tubes of a dying humanity comes the first of a race of gods.

(Broderick 1995: 11–12)

Broderick considers these 'hilariously awful...blazing sequel to dwarves, indeed!', but there is a serious point, too. As he observes, it is 'one of the comforts of this list, for habituated readers', that 'the catlike mrem live in a world which is precisely *not* unique' (Broderick 1995: 12). Many fans of SF seek out the comfort of the familiar, and mask that desire under the illusory rhetoric of difference, of 'catlike mrem' and their like.

This helps us draw these different definitions towards some sort of common conclusion. It seems that one of the axes of critical enquiry has to do with the degree of proximity of the 'difference' of SF to the world we live in: too removed and the SF text loses purchase, or becomes merely escapist; too close and it might as well be a conventional novel, it loses the force and penetration the novum can possess when it comes to providing newness of perspective. Balancing 'cognition' and 'estrangement', or the continuities and discontinuities of the SF text, becomes the index of success of the SF text. More than this, it seems that this balance is focused through the novum. In other words, implicit within these three definitions is a sense of SF as a *symbolist* genre, one where the novum acts as symbolic manifestation of something that connects it specifically with the world we live in. This is the position of one of the genre's most distinguished practitioners, Samuel Delany, who sees SF as 'a symbolist genre, because it seeks to represent the world instead of reproducing it' (Delany 1994: 123). Suvin, too, puts the emphasis here, describing SF as 'a symbolic system' which is 'centred on a novum which is to be cognitively validated within the narrative reality of the tale' (Suvin 1979: 80).

There are important differences in seeing SF as symbolist rather than allegorical. Symbolism opens itself up to a richness of possible interpretation, where allegory maps significance from one thing onto one other thing. More than this, any symbolist movement in literature, such as the late nineteenth-century movement of symbolist poetry, will tend to re-use a set corpus of symbols. M H Abrams lists some of the recurring icons of nineteenth-century symbolist writing, 'such as the morning and evening star, a boat moving upstream, winding caves, and the conflict between a serpent and an eagle' (Abrams 1985: 186). He goes on to quote symbolist poet Baudelaire to the effect that symbolism draws on 'the correspondences' between 'the spiritual and the natural world'. The point of SF, on the other hand, is to be less spiritual and more material, and accordingly this line of criticism enables us to look again at the limited range of nova deployed in most science fiction not as a narrow and exhausted set of cliches, but as a supple and wide-referencing body of material *symbols*. The catlike mrem, for example, can be seen less as a feeble rehashing of worn-out tropes and more as a fictional inhabiting – successful or not depending on the skill with which the author deploys these emblems – of a potent SF symbol of alienness.

The obvious point of contrast might be thought to be with a deliberately non-symbolist mode of writing, such as 'realism'. Realist fiction seeks to reproduce the experience of living in a particular milieu exactly and often exhaustively, and aims for a sense of documentary verisimilitude. But in a strange way, SF has more in common with realism than it has with other, more obviously imaginative, mainstream literatures. To elaborate this point it is worth noting that 'realism' is only one form of mainstream writing: much ordinary fiction introduces 'symbolic' devices, various imaginative strategies to provide 'discontinuities' with our experience of the world, without thereby becoming science fiction. But the textual function of these nova in SF sets them apart from other usage. In other words, SF gives us a unique version of the symbolist approach, one where the symbol is drained of transcendental or metaphysical aura and relocated back in the material world. For example, a 'realist' novel like Emile Zola's *Germinal* (1885) creates a sense of what it was actually like to live in a nineteenth-century French mining community by accumulating a great deal of accurately observed material detail. By contrast, a non-realist modernist novel like Virginia Woolf's *The Waves* (1931) is built around the stream-of-consciousness meanderings of its six characters. Instead of a large amount of realistic material detail, Woolf concentrates on certain recurring symbolic images, such as the sun rising and setting over a seascape, or the fin of a fish breaking the surface of the waves. Science fiction is symbolic, but it usually adopts the *realist* mode of an accumulation of detail, rather than the poetic and lyrical method of a writer like Woolf. To quote Suvin again, the symbolic novum 'has to be convincingly explained in concrete, even if imaginary, terms, that is, in terms of the *specific* time, place, agents, and cosmic and social totality of each tale'. Suvin goes on to note that 'this means that, in principle, SF has to be judged, like most naturalistic or "realistic" fiction and quite unlike [supernatural] horror fantasy, by the density and richness of objects and agents described in the microcosm of the text' (Suvin 1979: 80). The attention to detail and the density of the described reality in many SF texts mean that, very often, they read like realist novels; or perhaps a better phrase would be pseudo-realist. But the crucial point is that science fiction *reconfigures symbolism for our materialist age*.

It is this materialism, once again, that distinguishes the effectiveness of the SF use of symbol from the widespread use of symbolism in other literatures. To take another example: the trope of the 'invisible man' is one we might think of as a classic SF novum. H G Wells wrote a short novel on this theme in 1897. The difference between this SF text and Ralph Ellison's celebrated novel of Black American experience, also called *Invisible Man* (1952) – a book never described as SF – has to do with the operation of this novum in the text itself. Ellison's protagonist is invisible because people simply don't see him, and they don't see him because he is black. Ellison's point, in other words, is to express metaphorically, through the trope of the invisible man, the social invisibility and alienation that are part of the experience of being black in America. Wells's protagonist, on the other hand, is a scientist. His invisibility is specifically rationalised as the result of scientific research. The particular alienation experienced by Wells's invisible man stems from his own antisocial personality, which in turn is an expression of the way science denies common nature and humanity. Ellison's invisibility is a transcendent device, in the sense of being something that transcends or passes beyond conventional literary expectations; it is a means of metaphorically apprehending the experience of a whole group of people; Wells's is a concrete symbol of the dehumanisation of science, a particular coding of the very materiality of science's practice. Both have things to say about the real world, but the two works go about this in different manners.

THE SF NOVUM

It might make these issues of imaginative difference and continuity clearer to look at some specific examples of nova, in specific science-fiction texts. In each case it is not so much the ingenuity of the novum, or the strangeness of it, that is important; it is the symbolic purchase its point of difference provides on the world we live in.

One classic example of a small-scale novum – which deserves to be called classic because it crops up repeatedly in the criticism of SF – comes from Robert Heinlein's *Beyond This Horizon* (published as a book in 1948, although serialised in the magazine *Astounding Science-Fiction* in 1942). That novel starts with an office worker called Felix going to work. He arrives at his office, punches in a security code, and 'the door dilated'. All it takes is that little detail to evoke the particular response of the SF text. Here is an SF author and fan, Harlan Ellison, remembering his response:

And no discussion. Just 'the door dilated'. I read across it, and was two lines down before I realised what the image had been, what the words had called forth. A *dilating* door. It didn't open, it *irized*! Dear God, now I knew I was in a future world.

(Quoted in James 1994: 115)

Samuel Delany is also impressed by the way so slight a detail can shift our sensibilities into a different mode of world-perception. In the terms of 'realist fiction', says Delany, a phrase like 'the door dilated' is meaningless; but 'as SF – as an event that hasn't happened, yet still must be interpreted in terms of the physically explainable – it is quite as wondrous as Ellison feels it' (Delaney 1994: 228). For Delany the novum functions as a kind of trigger: it alerts the reader to the fact that she can't take things for granted, can't assume that the text she is reading reproduces the world in which she lives. The phrase compels the reader to re-orient her expectations. It is symbolic, in a useful way, of the point of entry of the reader into the SF text; it is a door through which we step into a different way of looking at things.

The difference that a concept such as a dilating door acquaints us with may seem trivial, but in an important sense it is not, because we can only make sense of a novum like this by placing it in context, and much of the context is something we have to imagine for ourselves. As a function of engaging our imagination in a thoroughgoing manner, the novum puts us in the position of rewriting, reconceptualising, the reality with which we are familiar – of constructing a whole and wholly different society, for instance, in which dilating doors might be a part. The more expertly the 'nova' are deployed, the more thorough this imaginative encounter with difference can be.

As with anything, this has its strong and weak forms in actual literary representation. John Meaney's *To Hold Infinity* (1998) is a richly-detailed evocation of a strange and complex future society; but the opening paragraph of this novel has the

sort of clotted awkwardness that SF texts sometimes employ to
suggest alterity:

> Flicker. Blindspin. Darkplunge. Golden light-fragments rip
> apart cobra's death-promise eyes. Laughter spirals. A muted
> discord: cymbals clash. Light, and light, kaleidoscopic fire-
> works burst above, below, drowning distant muttering.
>
> (Meaney, *To Hold Infinity* (1998): 7)

This attempts to articulate the physical novum of the novel, a
virtual-reality environment, in a particular written style that
strains after 'difference' from the more familiar conventions of
prose. Over-exerted like this, Meaney's style actually achieves
only bathos, the over-written excess of bad impressionist poetry.
Heinlein's dilating door, on the other hand, succeeds by virtue of
being low-key; the almost throwaway manner in which he introduces the detail is appropriate to the logic of the world he is
delineating. To a reader like Ellison the dilating door is startling
and wonderful, but we assume that for the people who inhabit
Heinlein's imaginary universe it is just a door. To put it in the
terms of the definitions of Suvin and Scholes, the fantastic perspective needs to be melded with the mundane in order to function effectively; Meaney's purple prose is too clumsily glittery to
manage this. The point of Broderick's observation about SF's 'de-
emphasis on fine writing' may be relevant here also; it is because
SF, by definition, deals with various fantastic things that it needs
to be balanced by a certain mundaneness in content and style. A
plain, functional style may serve usefully to offset the estranging
power of the SF novum.

A stronger, more thorough example of the sorts of thing I am
talking about can be found in the first chapter of Gwyneth
Jones's *White Queen* (1991), the James Tiptree Jr Award-winning
novel. This is set in the 2030s, in a grittily real crumbling series
of societies; the USA has recently become the USSA, the United

Socialist States of America, whereas the United States of Europe has become the dominant world power. A journalist, Johnny Guglioni, has been infected with a new strain of virus, one that is deadly both to human beings and to the semi-organic matter that is now at the core of electronic and computing equipment. He is living in what is effectively a quarantine in a small African state. It so happens that Johnny is amongst the first to encounter aliens from outer space. One of the most powerful aspects of Jones's deftly and intelligently written story is the way she relates this narrative of first contact both from the perspective of humans such as Johnny, and from the point of view of the aliens them-selves. In effect we are given two orders of alterity. It is left to our imaginations to fill in the sort of details that might plausibly underlie the political shift behind the change from 'USA' to 'USSA'; but at the same time we find ourselves reading a com-pelling but Other narrative, and trying to piece together the sort of consciousness for which this would be the most straightfor-ward way of looking at the world. Partly this happens on the level of what we might think of as 'inverted novum', which is to say the unfamiliarity of ordinary Earth things to the aliens.

> The cars had been hired, with unlimited mileage, in exchange for some baby toys.
> There had been consternation when, after carrying them for two days, the creatures collapsed in evident need of food. The captain's guardian had persuaded everyone to see the funny side. But the cost of the liquid food had curtailed their exploration.
>
> (Jones, *White Queen* (1991): 16)

The poet Craig Raine based a poem on this notion of the 'inverted novum': 'A Martian Sends a Postcard Home' (1979) is a text we might very well categorise as SF. Here, as in Jones's novel, ordinary things are represented as strange, such that a car is reconceptualised:

> Model T is a room with the lock inside –
> a key is turned to free the world
> for movement, so quick there is a film
> to watch for anything missed.
>
> (Raine, 'A Martian Sends a Postcard Home')

Or a telephone is 'a haunted apparatus [that] sleeps' and 'snores when you pick it up'. We might very well want to describe this poem, and the school of 'Martian' poetry it inspired, as science fictional.

But there are deeper layers of strangeness in the narrative of Jones's novel. The alien 'master at arms' is angry at the need to refuel the cars.

> 'Unlimited mileage!' he snarled, no less sore however often the liquid feed transaction was repeated.
>
> Agnès visited the sick and then went off by himself, taking care to remain in sight. He sat between the roots of a huge tree. The wooden fans made a house around him. He laid his own hand next to the hand of a fallen leaf. Even to the stubby fifth leaflet the shape was an echo, an echo of home; an echo of self. To give and to receive the Self with open palms. He shook hands with the fallen leaf, wondering what tiny faraway contact the local people felt. Perhaps none: they were not obliged to perceive him at all. He tasted the populated air, but none of its tiny messengers carried news for Agnès. The loneliness was dizzying. He took out his sketchpad and began to compose. *There*, the shape and texture of loneliness…and in loneliness a bodiless unity: the unity inescapable of the WorldSelf.
>
> (Jones, *White Queen* (1991): 17–18)

There is just enough that is familiar in this passage to make it possible for us to read it without becoming bewildered: a 'he' –

although with a female name – is sitting under a tree, contemplating a leaf, doing some 'sketching'. But the detail belongs to a very different conceptual pattern than the one we, as humans, are in the habit of applying to the world around us. As the novel continues, and we start to see things more from this alien perspective, its collation of 'home' and 'self', its tasting of the air, its bodiless sense of the WorldSelf, will introduce us to a different way of seeing the world around us.

By bringing together these two perspectives, Jones neatly reconceives the everyday world with which we thought we were familiar. The sheer strangeness of these two cultures to one another brings a sort of wisdom to the observation of even simple things. One of the aliens, Clavel, falls in love with Johnny, and in a lesser way Johnny reciprocates. Johnny also, more conventionally, falls in love with the heroine of the piece, the flawed and intriguing Braemar. Paralleling these two storylines allows Jones to delineate the immense comfort *and* the startling strangeness of what it is to be 'in love' – something that is given a jolting, brilliant and discomfiting dramatisation in the scene where Clavel makes love to Johnny.

> Clavel shucked off her underwear. The naked chicken-skin baboon crouched over him. It took his hand and buried it to the wrist in a fold that opened along its groin. The chasm inside squirmed with life. Part of its wall swelled, burgeoning outwards.
>
> '*Ah –*'
>
> The baboon clutched his wrist and worked its bellyfold up and down, its thighs slipped along his hips. It wasn't female after all, but a kind of hermaphrodite. Something slid out of the fold: an everted bag of raw flesh, narrowing to a hooked end. It was enormous. Johnny felt a jolt of horrible arousal, like the affectless clutch in the groin he'd get from a glimpse of violent pornography. Clavel's eyes were still fixed on his, *still*

sweet and childlike. Suddenly, he lost his nerve completely. He struggled and protested.

(Jones, *White Queen* (1991): 193)

This is close enough to a description of conventional human–human sex to call forth a visceral response in us, but it is grotesque enough to jolt us out of the merely conventional or conditioned response to 'the sex-scene'. There is genuine insight, I think, in the way Jones grants Johnny his horrible sexual arousal before the repulsion kicks in; mirroring the way this description of sex deploys just enough of the standard 'sex-scene' vocabulary, such as we might find in any shopping-and-sex novel: 'groin', 'chasm', 'swelled', 'thighs slipped along hips', whilst configuring them in such a disorienting manner, with a sprinkling of startling terms, such as 'chicken-skin baboon'. All of it positions us, the reader, in such a way as to prod us into rethinking our own attitudes to sex and love. It is also true that Jones takes the chance here, as many other female SF writers have done, to use the 'alien' as a way of inverting traditional gender stereotypes. Here, alien physiology means that a man can experience what it is to be 'raped' by someone of the opposite gender. This symbolic purchase on questions of gender in SF is examined at greater length in Chapter 3 of this book.

In other words, the key symbolic function of the SF novum is precisely the representation of the encounter with difference, Otherness, alterity. Not all these encounters with difference articulate as subtle or open a discourse as Jones manages, of course. A film such as the very successful *Lost in Space* (1998) represents a number of 'nova' and a variety of versions of difference; but at the same time it is so scared of difference that all possible manifestations of it need to be fully demonised and then utterly vanquished. Sameness in this movie is tightly defined as 'belonging to the Aryan family unit'; every good quantity encountered in the film either belongs to the family or is adopted by it – from the cute baby-like alien adopted by the family to the space pilot who is courting the blonde, blue-eyed, scientist's daughter. Everything that is not 'of the family' is represented as evil and threatening. The hidden agenda here, it seems to me, is racial. The Robinson family are so egregiously White that all representations of blackness become freighted with particular significance. When the fey, English villain is bitten by a being from a breed of half-organic, half-machine, alien monsters, he is metamorphosed into something terrible: 'evil always finds its true form', as Papa Robinson puts it. Its true form in this instance is that of a towering black man, who paces menacingly around the margins of the family, having perpetrated some unspeakable doom upon Will Robinson's mother and sister: 'I can still hear the screaming of the women,' says Will. The Robinsons are certainly encountering difference, but only in the limited sense of racial caricature, a violent, sexually predatory libel on black manhood. Difference, in other words, has been reduced to stereotype, and stereotype is always at the bottom of racism, sexism or any other bigotry. Ultimately, this black threat to the White family is flushed down a cosmic plughole like the rubbish he is represented as being, and the family is reunited to its stifling conformity. Here the symbolic field of signification seems racial, something that we examine in more detail in Chapter 4. This is one example of many in SF of a refusal to think through the implications of encountering difference. Not all SF is so crude or bigoted.

The problematic of this encounter with difference, the difficulty of representing the Other without losing touch with the familiar, becomes exactly the point of some of the most celebrated SF texts. It is possible to explore the strangeness and threat of the Other without surrendering to two-dimensional caricature of Otherness as evil. A classic example is Stanislaw Lem's novel *Solaris* (1961), set aboard a research station on another planet, a planet almost entirely covered with a strange ocean. It seems that this ocean is sentient, making the whole world a sort of giant brain. The scientist-protagonists of Lem's tale are trying to comprehend this unprecedented place; trying, in other words, to reduce it to the sameness of scientific explanation. But the world defies comprehension; it sends out hallucinations of people important to the scientists. The contact drives some of them mad. Snow, one of the occupants of the station, comes to an important realisation late in the novel, and anatomises the human urge to explore the universe:

> We don't want to conquer the cosmos, we simply want to extend the boundaries of Earth to the frontiers of the cosmos. For us, such and such a planet is as arid as the Sahara, another as frozen as the North Pole, yet another as lush as the Amazon basin...We are only seeking Man. We have no need of other worlds. We need mirrors.
>
> (Lem, *Solaris* (1961): 75–6)

The ocean-planet of Solaris, in its strangeness and unpredictability, denies this devouring urge to transmute all alterity into versions of sameness, and that is why the scientists cannot cope with it. The perfectly judged tone of uncanny uncertainty in Lem's novel, the way it consistently refuses the straightforward explanation of the characters' situation, precisely captures the way encountering the Other forces us to encounter ourselves, the way it can reveal things about ourselves which are intensely uncomfortable. 'We arrive here as we are in reality, and when the page is turned and that reality is revealed to us – that part of our reality which we would prefer to pass over in silence – then we don't like it any more' (p. 76).

DIFFERENCE

What these various definitions of SF have in common, then, is a sense of SF as in some central sense about the encounter with difference. This encounter is articulated through a 'novum', a conceptual, or more usually material embodiment of alterity, the point at which the SF text distils the difference between its imagined world and the world which we all inhabit. For Scott McCracken, 'at the root of all science fiction lies the fantasy of alien encounter'. He adds that 'the meeting of self with other is perhaps the most fearful, most exciting and most erotic encounter of all' (McCracken 1998: 102). This serves as the basis of many critics' affection for the genre, the fact that SF provides a means, in a popular and accessible fictional form, for exploring alterity. Specific SF nova are more than just gimmicks, and much more than cliches: they provide a symbolic grammar for articulating the perspectives of normally marginalised discourses of race, of gender, of non-conformism and alternative ideologies. We might think of this as the progressive or radical potential of science fiction.

But it is not necessarily clear that SF is as positive a mode as this optimistic assessment suggests. Even if we set aside the more obviously retrograde examples of SF that introduce difference only to demonise it, such as *Lost in Space* mentioned earlier, some critics are not sanguine about the ability of the genre to access Otherness. Damien Broderick, for instance, wonders if SF does, 'above all else, write the narrative of the other/s?', but goes on to say that even if we take that 'in the spirit of description (though hardly of definition)' we still have to accept that 'SF writes, rather, the narrative of the *same, as* other' (Broderick 1995: 51). Could we argue that all these SF nova, from aliens to machines, are merely elaborations of a monolithic conception of Identity?

The demographics of the genre are not hopeful in this regard. Until recently, SF was dominated by a fan culture of young white males. Science fiction's tendency to fetishise technology, particularly military technology, and its reliance on stock types of character and plot that are often flat and caricaturing, surely limits its engagement with any meaningful comprehension of the marginal, of Otherness. But there are features of this readership that start to redeem it: the energy of youth, for example, has a part to play in constructing SF as, to quote Roger Luckhurst, 'an adolescent and exuberantly kinetic genre' (Luckhurst 1997: 4). Indeed, despite the strong attachment of SF to its own canonical conventions, and despite the fact that until recently most SF was produced and consumed by young white males, the genre has always had sympathies with the marginal and the different. Gary Westfahl admits that 'science fiction [is] regularly condemned as the quintessentially masculine genre, long written almost exclusively by and for young men, filled with muscle-bound macho heroes swaggering and bullying their way through the galaxy'. But, Westfahl argues, the reality is not at all like this, because in fact SF has what he calls a 'feminine' aura. He itemises the way that American SF from the 1940s and 1950s – the so-called 'Golden Age' of SF – demonstrated remarkable sensitivities on the subjects of gender and racial diversity and contact, and asks:

> Why should this be, given the undeniable fact that most of the writers and readers were male? Well, the young nerds attracted to science fiction may have shared the gender and skin-colour of the era's dominant class, but in every other way they were alienated and marginalized members of society, dreaming of domed cities and Martian canals when most people longed for an idealized past and idolized [cowboy icons] Gene Autry and Andy Hardy. If, at that time, you read magazines with pictures of squid-like monsters and built miniature rockets in your backyard, you undoubtedly felt rejected, ridiculed, and out of place. Such people often bond with, and adopt the attitudes of, other members of society who feel rejected, ridiculed and out

of place. By this logic, one would expect to find in early science-fiction stories passionate arguments against prejudice and racism, celebrations of oppressed workers struggling against evil bosses, and proto-feminist tracts applauding the abilities and sentiments of women. And if you look carefully, you will find, in the science fiction of the 1930s and thereafter, numerous examples of all the above.

(Westfahl 1999: 32)

Reading SF, in other words, is about reading the marginal experience coded through the discourses of material symbolism; which is to say, it allows the symbolic expression of what it is to be female, or black, or otherwise marginalised. SF, by focusing its representations of the world not through *reproduction* of that world but instead by figuratively symbolising it, is able to foreground precisely the ideological constructions of Otherness. In other words, in societies such as ours where Otherness is often demonised, SF can pierce the constraints of this ideology by circumventing the conventions of traditional fiction.

PREDICTION AND NOSTALGIA

The difficulties of defining SF with which this chapter opened are, in part, a function of the sheer number of SF texts that need to be brought beneath the bar of any notional inclusive definition. Where SF once upon a time constituted a small body of texts – nearly all of them novels and short stories – which most fans could be expected to have read, nowadays SF texts are impossibly legion. Scott McCracken points out that 'Science Fiction is enormously popular. It accounts for one in ten books sold in Britain, and in the United States the number is as high as one in four' (McCracken 1998: 102). John Clute has pointed out that the number of texts classified as SF has ballooned since the early years of the twentieth century. According to Clute, even at the height of the 'Golden Age' the number of separate novels published as science fiction was a few hundred. Nowadays, taking together science fiction and fantasy, thousands of novels are published each year. Now, 'what was once a field [has] become the Mississippi Delta'. In Clute's opinion, if Golden Age SF could be perceived as 'a *family of books* which created (and inhabited) a knowable stage (or matrix) of possible worlds', then contemporary SF has exploded that family: 'no longer could an ostensible definition of SF...even begin to match the corrosive intricacies of the exploded genre' (Clute 1995: 17–18).

SF, then, clearly constitutes a wide range of varying discourses, so wide a range indeed that it becomes difficult to assert that all the different manifestations of 'SF' actually belong under the one umbrella term: not merely in terms of genre or mode, from short stories, novels, films, TV shows, comics, video games, pop music and so on, but in the broader sense of cultural discourse. Talking about NASA's space programme, or the present construction of the International Space Station, automatically, it seems, inhabits the idiom of SF; and the number of New Age or mystical belief-systems that have replaced conventional religion with a belief in one or another SF prop is remarkable, from abduction-enthusiasts who believe the Earth to be in the care of spiritually intense aliens, to cults who practise mass suicide in the belief that their souls will be carried away by an alien spacecraft hidden in a comet.

This was not always the case. In the so-called 'Golden Age' of science fiction, from the late 1930s through to the early 1960s, the term 'Science Fiction' had a greater degree of coherence. It referred to a particular body of texts that were, specifically, founded in science and the extrapolation of science into the future. Hugo Gernsback, founder of a number of influential SF magazines, inserted an editorial into the first number of his *Science Wonder Stories* (June 1929) in which he declared his 'policy' to be the publishing of 'only such stories that have their basis in scientific laws as we know them, or in the logical deduction of new laws from what we know'. He went so far as to announce that a panel of experts would judge the scientific correctness of stories submitted to the magazine. But there has been a shift in the role of the scientific novum; it now connects its readership less with a particular discourse of 'science' and rather, as I have been arguing, with a materialist, symbolic fiction for reconsidering the world. The balance, to re-use Scholes's distinction, has shifted towards the fabulation and away from the structural. As we have seen, the term 'science fiction' today suggests an imaginative fiction in which one or more of the contemporary constraints upon the business of living are removed or modified. John Clute sees 1957 as the significant historical moment, with the launch of the Russian satellite Sputnik.

> There may have been a time, in the morning of the world, before Sputnik, when the empires of our SF dreams were governed according to rules neatly written out in the pages of *Astounding*, and we could all play the game of a future we all shared, readers, writers, fans...But something happened. The future began to come true.
>
> (Clute 1995: 17)

This has something to do with a certain shift in cultural sensibilities. Space flight changed from being a thing of a gleamingly imagined future to being *real*, and then went on to pass that by and become, as it is nowadays, a thing of the *past*. A film such as Ron Howard's *Apollo 13* (1996) illustrates this neatly enough. It is a film about the adventures of the crew of a spaceship, off on a perilous mission, who have to battle with near-fatal malfunction, and accordingly it is a film that follows a standard SF trajectory, one seen in such classic films as *2001: A Space Odyssey* (1968) and *Dark Star* (1974). But this is a text that looks *backwards*, not forwards. The key thing, it seems to me, is less that the film is 'true'

– although, of course, it is – but that the film is so specifically *historical*. The astonishing special effects that recreate what lift-off in a Saturn 5 and a journey through space must have been like, are paralleled in the film by a precise recreation of the early 1970s milieu that is the setting for the picture. Watching *Apollo 13* is an experience that parallels more straightforwardly science-fictional films in interesting ways; but watching it also creates an acute awareness that 'going to the Moon' was something our ancestors did, not something we do today or are going to do in the future.

What *Apollo 13* does, in fact, is epitomise an important argument about SF made by several critics: that, although many people think of SF as something that looks to the future, the truth is that most SF texts are more interested in the way things *have been*. SF uses the trappings of fantasy to explore again age-old issues; or, to put it another way, the chief mode of science fiction is not prophecy, but *nostalgia*. That SF is not prophetic seems clear enough. There have been hundreds of thousands of SF texts throughout the twentieth century, but only very rarely – statistically no more than would be expected by the operations of chance – have any of those texts accurately predicted anything. Jules Verne predicted that men would fly to the Moon, blasting off from a location very close to Cape Canaveral in Florida; but he also thought that firing capsules out of cannons would be a good way of propelling people on this space voyage, when in fact the suddenness of the acceleration would squash the astronauts like bugs. H G Wells predicted the inventions of tanks and aerial bombing. But he didn't anticipate computers, didn't realise that life in space would be weightless, and confidently predicted that a worldwide government of scientists and rational men would create a global utopia by the 1950s. SF prediction is wrong far more than it is right, but we needn't be embarrassed on this account, because the recent developments in 'Chaos Theory' have taught us that the business of accurate prediction in a chaotic

system like 'The World' is literally impossible. So, despite a surface attachment to 'the future', it seems clear that SF actually
enacts a fascination with the past for which 'nostalgia' is the best
description. *Star Wars* (1977) begins with the caption 'A Long
Time Ago in a Galaxy Far Away...'; and the action of that film
owes more to the past, and specifically to director George Lucas's
youth, than to any coherently imagined future. His spaceships are
more like warplanes, going off on sorties straight out of *633
Squadron* or *The Dam Busters* than spaceships: this is why they
make screaming and whooshing noises when flying though the
noiseless vacuum of space. A spaceship would be silent, but the
X-Wing fighters aren't really spaceships, they're Spitfires and P-
51s. Frank Herbert's *Dune* (1965), one of the most famous SF
novels of the postwar period, is also thoroughly grounded in this
retro-vision. Despite being set in the 211th century, it introduces
us to a world that owes more to a dream of Arabia in the Middle
Ages than to any future we can plausibly conceive: a world without computers or science, a religious, mystical and superstitious
world, a reactionary and intensely old-fashioned world. I could
run through all the classic SF texts in a similar fashion. Philip K
Dick, seen by some as the most significant writer of SF in the
American postwar tradition, sets his books in a future that almost
exactly resembles 1950s American suburbia; Sheri Tepper's *Grass*
(1989) takes us to a distant future and a faraway planet in order
to express a storyline about Catholic guilt and fox-hunting. There
are a great many examples such as these.

Let me restate this point with another, extremely popular,
example. When the television series *Star Trek* was first aired in
the late 1960s, it worked hard to produce a design of futuristic
living that seemed plausibly of the future. But watching original-
series *Star Trek* today is an interesting temporally-dislocated
experience. It is a show that purports to be set in the 23rd century, and which includes many things – faster-than-light travel,
matter-transportation beams and so on – that are more advanced

than current technology. In that regard, it is 'futuristic'. But it is also, and at the same time, egregiously *dated*, in a rather quaint and unmistakably 1960s fashion. The clothes worn, the spaces inhabited, even the relative crudity of the special effects, constantly remind us that we are looking backwards, not forwards. I remember watching *Star Trek: the Next Generation* when that show first aired in the 1980s and being struck only by how suave and futuristic it looked. Watching re-runs, we are amazed by how extraordinarily dated and of its time it seems. The effect, I think, is to problematise in an interesting way our attitudes towards the temporal component of SF.

According to Fredric Jameson, the older cultural genres have 'spread out and colonised reality itself' (Jameson 1990: 371). This is more true of SF, I think, than any other genre. Just count the number of ways in which we can think about the world today that have been shaped by science fiction. The symbolic purchase of SF on contemporary living is so powerful, and speaks so directly to the realities of our accelerated culture, that it provides many of the conceptual templates of the modern Western world. The complex debates surrounding the genetic engineering of foodstuffs, for instance, enter popular consciousness in SF terms as 'Frankenstein foods'. The dangers of asteroid impact on our world find expression in such SF texts as the films *Deep Impact* (1997) and *Armageddon* (1998). Our feelings about computers have been rehearsed by every SF text that includes Artificial Intelligence; actual exploration of our solar system seems tame to us because our expectations have been raised by the thrills of the SF imagery; many people regard the trope of UFO abductions to be fact rather than science fiction, partly because of the expertness of SF texts such as *The X-Files*. As Istvan Csicsery-Ronay Jr puts it, 'SF has ceased to be a genre *per se*, becoming instead a mode of awareness about the world' (Csicsery-Ronay 1991: 308). SF does not project us into the future; it relates to us stories about our present, and more importantly about the past that has led to this present. Counter-intuitively, SF is a *historiographic* mode, a means of symbolically writing about history.

CASE STUDY: FRANK HERBERT, *DUNE* (1965)

This chapter will close with a more detailed reading of one of the classics of postwar SF, Frank Herbert's novel *Dune*. This novel is only one of the more obvious examples of the problematic way SF embodies alterity, the conceptual and material inhabitation of Otherness that also encodes issues relevant to the present: environmentalism, religion, culture and heroism. It is also very clearly rooted in a sense of the past.

Dune grew out of two separate ideas. After the fact, Herbert said:

> It [*Dune*] began with a concept: to do a long novel about the messianic convulsions which periodically inflict themselves on human societies. I had this idea that superheroes were disastrous for humans.
>
> (O'Reilly 1981: 38)

During the early 1960s Herbert began accumulating facts on world religions, trying to comprehend the psychology of mass phenomena, to understand why people gave themselves up to the juggernaut of messianic myth. The second prompt to the story was more particularly rooted in Herbert's journalistic career. A newspaper commissioned him to go to Florence, Oregon, to write a feature story about a government project on the control of sand dunes. A real problem in some parts of the overgrazed Midwest, dunes would move under the pressure of wind, swallowing roads, houses, even whole towns. The traditional methods of dealing with them – building walls – had little effect; but 1957 saw a new approach, the fixing of dunes by planting them with hardy grasses, an 'ecological' approach to the question. Herbert found himself fascinated by the subject:

I had far too much for an article and far too much for a short story. So I really didn't know what I had – but I had an enormous amount of data and avenues shooting off at all angles to get more...I finally saw that I had something enormously interesting going on for me about the ecology of deserts, and it was, for a science fiction writer anyway, an easy step from that to think: What if I had an entire planet that was desert?

(O'Reilly 1981: 38)

These all-consuming dunes neatly embody the on-rolling, devouring force of messianic myth that is the theme of the novel. We can see, then, why Herbert seems to have decided to combine these two stories. 'I decided to put the two together because I don't think any story should have only one thread. I build on a layer technique, and of course putting in religion and religious ideas with ecological ideas you can play one against the other.' The effect of linking these two discourses in the novel is to make explicit the *symbolic* burden of the whole. Landscape, pared down to a singular quantity, acquires symbolic resonance that links it to the messianic theme. It encourages us to read past the surface of the novel, to explore its correspondences and ideological codings.

The novel as we have it is divided into three parts: Dune, Muad'Dib and The Prophet, which is a rough index of how Herbert orchestrates his components. Paul Atreides, the hero, comes to Dune as an outsider; he is born on the Earth-like planet Caladan and arrives on Arrakis (Dune) at the age of 16 with his father Duke Leto. This enables the first part of the book to introduce the world and culture of the desert planet, thus arranging our encounter with the difference through the device of the initiation of the protagonist. At the end of this first part, the evil Baron Harkonnen seizes the planet and murders Paul's father, forcing Paul to flee. The second part, which takes as its title the name Paul adopts among the Fremen, the desert dwellers, details his Lawrence-of-Arabia-style encounter with the ways of the desert tribes, his acceptance by the Fremen, his adoption of the position of ruler and his taking of a Fremen wife. The third section is where the religious strand takes centre stage; in terms of basic narrative the final third of the book is a return: Paul takes his revenge against Harkonnen and the Emperor and the book comes full circle.

In many senses, then, this is an old-fashioned book. As critic Timothy O'Reilly describes it: 'It is a heroic romance of the best kind. Good and evil are clear-cut. The growth of young Paul to a heroic figure who can snatch victory from overwhelming defeat is a growth in awareness and self-mastery, as well as power. What reader is not heartened when Paul triumphs over all the forces massed against him?' (O'Reilly 1981: 150). And, of course, the whole universe that Herbert creates is almost medieval in terms of its technological non-sophistication. To put it another way, the nostalgic cast of this novel inflects its representation of technology. Herbert's universe is one without much by way of machinery, and with nothing at all by way of thinking machines or computers: these were wiped out in the 'Butlerian jihad', 'the crusade against computers, thinking machines, and conscious robots' (Herbert, *Dune* (1965): 594). Generally speaking, most of the technology in this novel would not be out of place in a shop today. More particularly, there are only two areas in which *Dune* introduces items that we might think of as technological nova; and even these are compromised by the logic of the novel. One is interstellar travel, a necessary precondition for the book we might think; and yet this premise is explained not scientifically but mystically, with the spaceships depending upon pilots who are Spice-addicted (drug-addicted) mutants and therefore no longer human: 'The Guildsman was an elongated figure, vaguely humanoid with finned feet and hugely fanned membranous hands...his tank's vents emitted a pale orange cloud rich with the smell of the geriatric spice, melange' (Herbert 1967, 11). The

Spice and the Guildsman's mutated form enable him to somehow sense his path through 'foldspace', the SF-standard hyperspace, and guide a spaceship on its path. We are given no sense of the mechanics or technology of space flight apart from this peculiar quasi-religious staging; and there are no scenes set in space in *Dune* or the next three of its sequels (*Dune Messiah*, *Children of Dune* and *God Emperor of Dune*). The effect of this is to defamiliarise technology, to characterise it as 'magic' or 'religion' rather than quotidian machinery.

The other technological novum of the novel has to do with weaponry and war. We are introduced to a variety of alarming-sounding weapons in the novel – the 'Lasgun', a 'continuous wave laser projector', the 'Maula Pistol' with its poisoned darts, the five-centimetre-long Hunter-Seeker, 'a common assassination weapon that every child of royal blood learned about at an early age. It was a ravening sliver of metal guided by some near-by hand and eye. It could burrow into moving flesh and chew its way up nerve channels to the nearest vital organ' (Herbert, *Dune* (1965): 84). We also learn about Defensive Shields, which can be worn individually or arranged about buildings or whole cities, that 'will permit entry only to objects moving at slow speeds' and that have rendered the use of lasguns almost irrelevant, since a lasgun fired at a shield will result in 'explosive pyrotechnics' powerful enough to destroy both attacker and defender. But at the same time that Herbert is detailing these fancy war technologies, he is undercutting the futuristic burden. An early chapter sees Paul being trained in knife-fighting by the Atreides weapons-master Gurney Halleck. As with *Star Wars* (a film which, as several critics have noted, owes a great deal to *Dune*), a fascination with the toy-like ingenuity of machine technology is ultimately undercut by a deeper sense of satisfaction at a retro-defined sense of chivalric conflict. This happens on a personal level, so that the battles in *Dune* are fought by individuals with knives and swords; this includes two crucial scenes, Paul's fight with the Freman Jamis that establishes his place in the Sietch, and his climactic knife-fight with the evil Feyd-Rautha. But it also happens on a larger one: Paul eventually defeats the Emperor and captures the planet by resorting to antique weaponry, namely atomic bombs, that had been long outlawed.

In both these senses, then, *Dune* is a novel built around a sense of stepping backwards; it portrays a world supposedly immensely removed from us in time and space, thousands of light years away and in the year 10,190, but actually intensely familiar to us because of its groundedness in a medieval Arabian paradigm *made* familiar to us through literature and film (particularly through David Lean's film of *Lawrence of Arabia*, 1962). Its familiarity depends upon its old-fashionedness, and the old-fashioned heroic-romance storyline and old-fashioned props only reinforce this. Nor, to be clear about this, am I suggesting that this is entirely a bad thing. It helps explain why *Dune* is so effective: the sense of detail and completeness, of an imagined universe that is larger than the bits that happen to be presented to us in the novel, gives the book a breadth most novels, let alone SF novels, lack; and that sense of verisimilitude in turn depends upon the fact that the book is rooted in actual experience. To mention an example from a parallel mode of writing, Fantasy, J R R Tolkien does something similar in *The Lord of the Rings* by writing a personal and idiosyncratic mythology that is firmly rooted in the actual mythologies of northern Europe.

But this begs certain questions about *Dune* in respect of its encounter with Otherness or the alien. A world so familiar, with so little that is radically new to us, could easily be a stale and imaginatively poor world. This situation is made more acute by the way Herbert uses a binarism at least as old as the novel itself to propel his story onwards. What I mean by this is that the motor for this story is a straightforward moral battle, a battle between good and evil. The good is the family Atreides, and Paul in particular; and their 'goodness' is emphasised by a hundred details – they are humane, civilised, cultured, intelligent. When Paul's mother, the Lady Jessica, realises that the physician Yueh's wife had been killed by Harkonnen, her reaction is one of instinctive compassion: ' "forgive me," Jessica said. "I do not mean to open an old wound." And she thought *Those animals!*' (Herbert, *Dune* (1965): 79). In a key scene Duke Leto, flying over the desert to inspect one of his own Spice-mining operations, saves the crew from attack by the ravenous giant sandworms that infest the desert. The ecologist Kynes, watching the bravery and humanity of the action, is impressed despite himself:

*This Duke was concerned more over the men than he was over the spice. He risked his own life and that of his son to save the men. He passed off the loss of a spice crawler with a gesture. The threat to men's lives had him in a rage. A leader such as that would command fanatical loyalty...*Against his own will and all previous judgments, Kynes admitted to himself: *I like this Duke.*

(Herbert, *Dune* (1965): 150)

After the Duke is betrayed and killed, Paul survives by virtue of physical strength and bravery, ingenuity and determination. He is unambiguously heroic.

By way of contrast, the 'evil' half of the moral equation is painted in utterly despicable colours. The villains of the piece come close to caricature. 'Beast' Rabban, with his unspeakable (and unspoken) wickednesses; Feyd-Rautha, who is fond of fighting to the death in – once again – old-fashioned 'Roman Empire' gladiatorial-style combats, but, so as not to risk getting hurt, only ever fights carefully chosen opponents who are drugged beforehand to render them almost helpless; the Padishah Emperor Shaddam IV, a two-dimensional mixture of decadent obsession with the splendour of court and a brutally oppressive tyranny, enforced by his SS-like shock troops the Sardaukar. But worst of all is the grotesque figure of the Baron Harkonnen, and it is the Baron's overweight body that is the most obvious focus for the limitations of the representation of Otherness in *Dune*.

Harkonnen is a very effective villain, but his very villainy is a direct function of his Otherness. He is, to begin with, foreign: his name (Vladimir Harkonnen) suggests that he is coded as Russian: as O'Reilly points out, 'the Russian sound' of the Baron's name 'was clearly meant to engage our prejudices – which, it must be remembered, were much stronger when *Dune* was written in the early sixties than they are now' (O'Reilly 1981: 55). He is physically grotesque, enormously fat, so obese that he can only move around with 'suspensors' strapped to his body to carry most of its weight. It is his physical repulsiveness that is most consistently dwelt upon. His first appearance is crudely if effectively orchestrated, as he plots the downfall of the Atreides house in the shadows like a Bond villain: 'a relief globe of the world, partly in shadows, spinning under the impetus of a fat hand that glittered with rings' (Herbert, *Dune* (1965): 25). The point of this goes beyond a class-based characterisation of Harkonnen as 'decadent', although he is that. The response is more visceral. 'As he emerged from the shadows, his figure took on dimension – grossly and immensely fat' (p. 33). But in addition to being coded as repulsive because *racially* and *physically* different to the heroic 'norm' established by Paul, the Baron is also negatively portrayed as *sexually* different. This amounts to a crudely worked-through homophobia. A few pages after presiding over the deaths of Yueh and Piter with utter cold-bloodedness, and after consigning Arrakis to, as he thinks, sixty years of tyranny, Harkonnen is explicitly compared to the Devil, or at least the Beast of Revelation: 'Leto suddenly recalled a thing Gurney Halleck had once said, seeing a picture of the Baron: *And I stood upon the sand of the sea and saw a beast rise out of the sea…and upon his hands the name of blasphemy*' (p. 213). And at the end of the same chapter, apparently as a means of climactically reinforcing just how repulsive and despicable the

Baron is, we discover not only that he is homosexual but that he has lustful designs upon Paul Atreides himself:

> 'I'll be in my sleeping chambers,' the Baron said. 'Bring me that young fellow we bought on Gamont, the one with the lovely eyes. Drug him well. I don't feel like wrestling.'
> 'Yes, m'Lord.'
> The Baron turned away... *Yes*, he thought. *The one with the lovely eyes, the one who looks so much like the young Paul Atreides.*

> (Herbert, *Dune* (1965): 219)

Perhaps this was less marked in the more automatically homophobic 1960s; today it strikes an odd note. Why should the fact that Harkonnen is gay, or that he finds Paul attractive – Paul is certainly presented as being attractive – be in itself a reason to detest him? The point reflects uneasily, I think, on just how old-fashioned a novel *Dune* is, how unquestioned its moral schema and therefore its prejudices are. We are given a world of few, if any, moral ambiguities; right is clearcut and wrong signals its presence by being repulsive or effeminate or, indeed, both. Otherness, or 'the alien', is in the first instance represented through the perspective of a tribal culture based on the medieval Bedouin, for whom any person or thing from outside the tribe was to be treated with suspicion and even hatred. This might be thought fatally to compromise the novel's ability to represent the alien. The characters we encounter are, if anything, rather two-dimensional, rather ordinary, familiar to us from countless other novels.

But there is one crucial novum in *Dune* which steps outside the restrictive binary of 'good versus evil' in which much of the rest of the novel is trapped: the giant sandworms, the enormous serpent-like alien creatures that are crucial to the ecology of the planet. And here I think Herbert does something very clever. He is able to throw the alien into relief against a background of familiarity, and therefore make the Otherness all the more striking, all the more powerful. This is why the giant sandworms stand out so powerfully in the imagination of the readers of *Dune*.

The sandworms live beneath the surface of the sands of the desert; non-sentient, but drawn to the pockets of the drug 'Spice', and to any regular sound made on the surface. Most of the inhabitants of the planet fear these monstrous, alien beasts; but it is a sign of his religious destiny that Paul is able to see past this shallow response. The worm is connected with Paul's acceptance by the Fremen, because he must learn to ride one as they do to become truly one of the tribe. As he faces this test, the Otherness of the beast becomes beauty: *'Come up you lovely monster*, he thought. *Up. You hear me calling'* (p. 463). The enormous worms are segmented, and a rider can compel them to stay on the surface of the desert by prising back the edge of one of these segments with a grappling hook; rather than get sand under its skin, the worm will carry the rider over the surface of the desert. Once he succeeds in mounting the worm, Paul revels in his power:

> He felt exultant, like an emperor surveying the world. He suppressed a sudden urge to cavort there, to turn the worm, to show off his mastery of this creature.
>
> (Herbert, *Dune* (1965): 464)

This may be poorly written ('cavort' is an especially ugly touch), but it does at least dramatise the symbolic pertinence of this novum. At the book's climax, the Fremen army ride into battle, and victory, on the back of the sandworms: Paul turns his empire from dream to reality. In other words, we understand what epistemological riddle the worms stand for: what they stand for symbolically. They represent Power, the power to devour and terrify. They represent man's power over nature in that they are ridden by men; they represent the power of the army as they carry the

Fremen troops to victory; and most important of all, for the universe Herbert has created, they represent political power on the grand scale, because they are specifically implicated in the creation of Spice, the drug on which all political power rests.

It is the sandworms that dominate *Dune*. They are the most potent and the most memorable of Herbert's inventions in the novel, the thing readers carry away with them. And it seems clear to me that the reason for this is that it is in the figure of the sandworms that Herbert found his most powerful and least flawed embodiment of alterity. The worms are utterly different from us, or from anything we know; and that they are located in a world that is familiar enough from cultural representations of medieval Arabia only serves to highlight the beautiful strangeness of the beasts. They embody alienness in themselves, as well as carrying with them the connotation of the strangeness of the desert landscape that Herbert evokes so well. And more than this, as I have been arguing, they encode the operation of power as itself strange, *not* as natural or ordinary but as outlandish. It is this level of signification that renders *Dune* an effective novel, I think; that underlies all the cruder ethical binarism of good versus evil that otherwise lumpishly separates and condemns alterity in the text. There is, in other words, enough genuine encounter with difference in this novel, particularly the striking sandworms and the intriguing Spice, to carry the text beyond its otherwise disfiguring condemnations of racial, physical and sexual difference. And as a novel it can put together an oblique and suggestive coding of the operation of Power as the revaluation of all value, the encounter with Otherness.

The mysticism of *Dune* coalesces around gender distinctions. A mystical sect that is exclusively female, the Bene Gesserit Sisterhood, has been operating a breeding policy for thousands of years, hoping to produce a specific individual with tremendous powers of insight into the future and the past. Although this mystic spirituality is something they reserve for women, it seems that this messiah-figure, called in the novel the Kwisatch Haderach, can only be a man. In other words, potent though the female purchase on these mystical abilities is, there is something a woman lacks that this man has, something that will empower him to do things that a woman cannot do. On a symbolic level, it seems clear that there is some transcendental signifier being alluded to here. As the novel progresses, and it becomes apparent that Paul is indeed the Kwisatch Haderach, his triumphant Power-symbolic experience on the unavoidably phallic sand-worms takes on the connotations of a particular discourse of gender – of masculine gender. This in turn connects the symbolism of this novel to lived experience. Its symbolic nova open up fertile avenues of interpretation that work into the discourses of Power and masculinity. The limitations of the novel's ethical schema can be seen in this light as a critique of the narrowness of masculine, phallic power; the anxieties it expresses about male homosexuality being nothing more than the inherent contradictions of the masculinist ideology. SF, according to Peter Lev in *The Cyborg Handbook*, is 'a privileged vehicle for the presentation of ideology. Because it is less concerned than other genres with the surface structure of social reality, science fiction can pay more attention to the deep structures of what is and what ought to be' (Gray *et al.* 1995: 30). *Dune* provides a good example of this.

2

THE HISTORY OF SCIENCE FICTION
FROM BEGINNINGS TO THE 1960s

ORIGINS

The identification of a point of origin for science fiction is as fiercely contested a business as defining the form. Different critics have their own favourite jumping-off points: some go back no further than a hundred years, to H G Wells and Jules Verne, giving SF as a genre a youthfulness to fit its supposedly juvenile, forward-fixated profile. Others insist on searching out 'fantastic' or 'science-fictional' elements in literature as ancient as literature is itself. There are journeys to the Moon or heroic protagonists seeking out new worlds and strange new civilisations in the oldest epics of human culture, from the ancient Sumerian *Epic of Gilgamesh* (written perhaps in 2000 BC) onwards. This presents us with two broad approaches to the question of origins, and the difference between these two approaches focuses different ways of understanding the nature of SF. Stress the relative youth of the mode, and you are arguing that SF is a specific artistic response to a very particular set of historical and cultural phenomena: for instance, that SF could only have arisen in a culture experiencing the Industrial Revolution, or one undergoing the metaphysical anxieties of what nineteenth-century philosopher Friedrich Nietzsche called 'the Death of God'. Stress the antiquity of SF, and you are arguing instead that SF is a common factor across a wide range of different histories and cultures, that it speaks to something more durable, perhaps something fundamental in the human make-up, some human desire to imagine worlds other than the one we actually inhabit.

So, for example, much science-fiction criticism talks about the origins of SF in the nineteenth century, with a few select texts from earlier epochs instanced as precursors. SF critic Peter Nicholls thinks that 'SF proper requires a consciousness of the scientific outlook', and that 'a cognitive, scientific way of looking at the world did not emerge until the 17th century, and did not percolate into society at large until...the 19th'. He adds that 'there is no sense at all in which we can regard SF as a genre conscious of *being* a genre before the 19th century' (Clute and Nicholls 1993: 567–8). Similarly, Brian Aldiss sees Mary Shelley's *Frankenstein* (1818) as the first SF text; the originary scientific fable about the power of the scientist to create, matched with the unforeseeable nature of the consequences of that creation. For a more explicitly scientific pedigree it is common enough to read critical histories of SF that begin, after a cursory mention of a few earlier texts, with the writing of H G Wells and Jules Verne. Both these writers have been called 'The Father of Science Fiction' (only in an SF tale could a child have two fathers and no mother). Certainly the influence of both Wells and Verne on the development of SF in the twentieth century has been enormous.

On the other hand there are critics who like to cite earlier texts. A popular example of proto-SF is Lucian, a Syrian novelist who wrote in the second century AD. In his *True History*, the ship in which the narrator is sailing is caught up by a hurricane and hurled into the sky, from where it sails on to the Moon. In another Lucian work, the *Icaromenippus*, the protagonist uses the wings of a vulture and an eagle in order to fly to the Moon. Sometimes even earlier texts are mentioned. The *Epic of Gilgamesh* and the Bible are two works sometimes mentioned, because they mix passages aimed at a recreation of everyday life in terms we might think loosely of as 'realist' with scenes that are fantastic, impossible, supernatural or miraculous. We are not in the habit, perhaps, of thinking of the Bible as science fiction; but in so far as it does provide us with the myths with which our culture encounters Otherness, the label has a certain appropriateness. This is not quite to say, though, that the Bible provides us with specific SF scenes or images. Of course, there have been people eager to read something like the Biblical account of Jacob's Ladder in SF terms, as a ladder let down by a hovering flying saucer, for example; but it is hard to see this sort of interpretative action as anything other than an imaginative imposition. We need to bring in a deal of belated imaginative furniture to posit a flying saucer hovering over the desert; and whilst this fact doesn't invalidate a reading along those lines, it does indicate a critical posture from within the framework of SF, and accordingly doesn't identify the origins of that framework. In SF terms, the important thing about a work like *Gilgamesh*, one of humanity's oldest pieces of literature, is that in telling the story of a hero who encounters monsters and supernatural goings-on it provides us with the metaphorical basis of an encounter with difference. The monsters of such a work function as nova, in a manner of speaking.

Interestingly *Star Trek: the Next Generation* structured a whole episode ('Darmok at Jilad') around a retelling of the *Gilgamesh* epic. This is a highly regarded *Trek* episode, and with good reason. It constitutes an efficient symbolic representation of the coming to terms precisely with a radical instance of difference. In the 'Darmok' episode the human Captain of the *Enterprise*, Jean-Luc Picard, encounters a wholly new alien life form, so different to us that their language cannot be translated by the most advanced translation programmes of the Federation. The point of drawing the parallel with the *Epic of Gilgamesh* seems to be that, in their own way, just so did the heroes of ancient epic encounter radical difference, titled variously 'gods' or 'monsters', located in strange new locations such as 'the heavens' or 'the underworld'. In 'Darmok' it turns out that the aliens can communicate only with metaphors; in fact their speech is so wholly metaphorical that even when the specific words and constructions have been translated into English, they remain meaningless because the metaphorical content is unknown. We might refer to somebody as 'a Romeo', meaning that they are metaphorically a Romeo in the sense of being like Shakespeare's character, but if the metaphorical usage is not understood the phrase does not work. Gradually, Picard learns the cultural underpinnings of the alien language, and so starts to communicate. The alien refers Picard to a myth from his culture, a myth about a warrior called Darmok that provides the content of the linguistic structures that define its form of communication. By way of reciprocation, Picard tells the alien the story of Gilgamesh, since it is one of the myths that is metaphorically part of our language, our discourse. This is to say that references to these sorts of myth lie behind much of our communication: calling somebody 'a Romeo' will only be meaningful if the reference to Shakespeare's *Romeo and Juliet* is understood. The tension between the literal – for instance, science – and the metaphorical – fiction – is particularly appropriate to SF. This episode of *Trek* elegantly expresses the underlying symbolic purchase of the 'language' of science fiction itself. It goes elegantly to the heart of the metaphorical power of SF; the way it tends to signify more than itself, to open itself to multiple significations.

This in turn suggests a characterisation of SF as a kind of meta-language, one which is spoken more or less competently depending on how much of the symbolic and metaphoric content of the tropes is understood. Like the alien's language in the

'Darmok' episode, speaking 'science fiction' well depends upon understanding the references and allusions to famous SF texts. Certainly it is hard to read contemporary SF without some sense of the history of the genre, if only because so many SF writers today allude to and rework the canonical texts of the past. A reader fresh to the genre might enjoy Kim Stanley Robinson's *Mars* trilogy on the level of story, character and style; but an SF fan notices layers of meaning beyond the surface in the detailed impacting of reference to the SF history of stories about Mars, from H G Wells and Edgar Rice Burroughs's *Barsoom* books up to the present day. In *Red Mars*, the first book of the Mars trilogy, the majority of settlements on the planet are named after SF authors, 'Burroughs', 'Sheffield' and 'Clarke'. Because the Mars day is not divisible neatly by Earth hours there is a period of twenty minutes at midnight when the clocks don't run; Robinson calls this gap the 'Martian time slip', referring literally to what it is but also slyly quoting the title of one of Philip Dick's most famous novels, *Martian Time-Slip*. A reader knowledgeable in the history of SF picks up these references in a way a new reader cannot. Indeed, SF author and critic Samuel Delany thinks that this critical mass of canonical SF texts gives twentieth-century SF a generic coherence that cannot be applied to earlier 'fantastic' writing. He dismisses the claims of works such as Thomas More's *Utopia* (1516), Kepler's *Somnium* (1634), Cyrano de Bergerac's fantastical *Voyages to the Moon and Sun* (1656), or even a late-Victorian example of utopian writing such as Edward Bellamy's *Looking Backward* (1888). Delany insists that 'that whole model of the "history of SF" is ahistorical. More, Kepler, Cyrano, and even Bellamy would be absolutely at sea with the codic conventions by which we make sense of the sentences in a contemporary SF text.' He goes on to suggest that 'pedagogic snobbery' is behind the urge to construct 'these preposterous and historically insensitive genealogies with Mary Shelley as our grandmother or Lucian of Samosata as our great-great grandfather' (Delany 1994: 26).

The sharpness of tone exhibited by Delany is revealing, however. Many SF fans can become very heated when it comes to definition and history. This gives the symbolism of most SF texts an interesting double element. A text like Robinson's novel exists in a context of imaginative symbolism, focused on its novum, which relates the world; but it simultaneously exists in a literary/SF context, where much of the narrative refers not literally to its imagined world, not symbolically to the real world in which it was created or into which it is received, but metaphorically to the fan-beloved traditions of SF writing itself. The self-referentiality of the metaphorical aspect of SF goes some way towards giving this diverse body of writing its sense of internal coherence. Even a text such as the one you are reading depends upon a certain metaphorical ambition. To identify a 'point of origin' for this enormously expanding mode of writing seems to allude to another scientific, if not explicitly science-fictional, metaphor of beginnings: the Big Bang. It is fair, I think, to call the Big Bang science-fictional instead of scientific, because it remains a hypothesis extremely difficult to test experimentally; it is, in other words, an imaginative construction elaborated from a series of scientifically rigorous premises. We cannot 'know' that the universe began this way, but we also cannot deny the imaginative potency of the conception. In other words, the science of thinking about the Big Bang draws on a rich body of scientific writing; but the *imaginative* conception owes more to certain literary traditions, most obviously the religious and mythical traditions such as the Jewish/Christian scriptures: 'And the [universe] was without form, and void...and [God] said "let there be light", and there was light.' Indeed, it could be argued that SF has been so successful a mode of cultural production that it has thoroughly colonised the world of 'science', that there isn't any longer a 'science' as applied to the real world that is distinct from 'science fiction'. When science makes any sort of imaginative attempt to apprehend the world of lived experience it becomes SF. A page of mathematical formulae may be science, but the scientific conception of how things are on the event-horizon of a black hole to which those formulae refer becomes SF, once it is located in the discourses of everyday humanity. There is a close relationship between, first, the metaphors used *by* SF, such as 'the world is like a spaceship', in a novel like Brian Aldiss's *Nonstop*; second, the metaphors that *define* SF, such as the parallel between SF writing as a mode, beginning with a single text, the *Epic of Gilgamesh*, say, or the Bible, or Mary Shelley's *Frankenstein*, and expanding outwards like the universe itself; and third, the metaphors that shape our appreciation of the world beyond our immediate experience, such as the billions of stars and phenomena in the universe. Thinking metaphorically is thinking fictionally, however grounded in science those metaphors might be.

Another text often cited as a starting place for SF is more promising in this sense. Thomas More wrote his *Utopia* in Latin in 1516, and it was translated into English in 1551. It describes an ideal society in which everybody coexists harmoniously, located on a fictional crescent-shaped island. The extent to which More was imaginatively creating a new type of society is also the extent to which this work, which is so thoroughly rational in its Renaissance aims as to include nothing fantastic or futuristic whatsoever, can be called proto-SF. It is partly satire on the short-comings of actual English society, partly a blueprint for a better way of ordering society; and in this latter capacity it is couched in exclusively *possible* terms. It might be argued that the mere act of creating this alternative world renders the work science-fictional, but as novum, More's imaginative version of sixteenth-century England actually works to reinforce sameness. The island is separated from the world, impregnable to attack, and in an important way it depends upon having the rest of the world as the place where the evils and problems of the world are located, so that the 'goodness' of the Utopian realm can be concentrated in one place. *Utopia* is not therefore a text concerned with the encounter with Otherness.

One of the advantages of a focus on SF as a literature about the encounter with difference, and particularly the concretisation of that encounter, is that it provides a new perspective on the origins of this durable genre. My own nomination for the ur-text of SF comes somewhere between the 'antiquity of SF' school and the 'SF as a distinctly modern phenomenon' school. I do consider SF to be modern, not ancient; and by modern I mean 'post-Romantic', that is to say coming after the revaluation of culture and metaphysics associated with the Romantic period, roughly 1780–1830. In particular, SF has much in common with the sub-genre of 'Gothic fiction' characteristic of this period. As author and critic Brian Aldiss argues, 'Science fiction was born from the Gothic mode, is hardly free of it now. Nor is the distance between the two modes great. The Gothic emphasis was on the distant and the unearthly' (Aldiss 1973: 18). The critic M H Abrams lists the conventions frequently found in the Gothic, a mode frequently set 'in a gloomy castle replete with dungeons, subterranean passages, and sliding panels' which 'made bountiful use of ghosts, mysterious disappearances and other sensational and supernatural occurrences...their principal aim was to evoke chilling terror' (Abrams 1985: 74). But the Gothic was only a symptom of the larger literary and cultural phenomenon known as 'Romanticism', and in particular it is the primacy of notions of the Imagination and the Sublime associated with Romantic writing that sets the agenda for the development of SF. Not only Romantic poets like William Blake and Percy Bysshe Shelley, but also writers of Gothic novels like Horace Walpole and Mary Shelley, foregrounded 'the Imagination' as the key artistic faculty. And it was with the deployment of Imagination, which we can read for our purposes as 'the creative entering into the possibilities of the fantastic, the unknown and the other-than-the-everyday', together with the awe-inspiring splendour of 'the Sublime' – which today is behind what is sometimes called 'Sense of Wonder SF' – that established the artistic framework within which all SF writers today work.

But this does not mean that I want to locate the origins of SF in Mary Shelley's *Frankenstein*, important though that text is for the development of SF, or even in the earlier work such as Percy Shelley's poetical *Queen Mab* (1813), where the protagonist travels around the solar system in a magic car, or William Blake's splendidly imaginative *Marriage of Heaven and Hell* (1793). There is SF in nascent form in all these texts, I think; but that SF germ is derived from an earlier text, one that had a uniquely powerful impact on Romanticism in general: John Milton's *Paradise Lost* (1674).

Broadly speaking, what the Romantics did with Milton's great epic was to shift the emphasis of reading. *Paradise Lost* tells the story of Adam and Eve in the garden of Eden; of their falling to temptation and eating the fruit of the Tree of the Knowledge of Good and Evil, and their expulsion from paradise. To frame this tale, taken straightforwardly enough from the Bible, Milton also tells the story of the fall of Lucifer from Heaven to a vividly realised Hell, where he becomes Satan; and of Satan's resolution to continue to oppose God by any means he can. Milton needs to do this to explain why Eve broke God's law over the matter of the tasty but fatal fruit: because she was tempted by Satan in the shape of a serpent. But it means that Milton is able to allow his imagination to roam throughout the whole of the solar system; to wonder, for example, whether a race of aliens inhabits the Moon:

> if land be there,
> Fields and inhabitants: her spots thou seest
> As clouds, and clouds may rain, and rain produce
> Fruits in her softened soil, for some to eat
> Allotted there; and [whether] other suns perhaps
> With their attendant moons thou wilt descry.
>
> (Milton, *Paradise Lost* (1993): 184)

Christian writer C S Lewis wrote a trilogy of SF novels

(*Perelandra*, *Out of the Silent Planet* and *That Hideous Strength*, 1938–45) based on this idea, that God had allotted different sorts of beings to each of the planets. But these kinds of details, or the various voyages of angels and devils through space to land, for instance, on the Sun – which Satan does, to discover it 'glowing iron with fire;/If metal, part seemed gold, part silver clear' (Milton, *Paradise Lost* (1993): 80) – are more likely to strike us as quasi-SF because we have been trained to read such things in the context of SF. There is something more important for our purposes in the poem's actual conception. Milton claimed its purpose was to 'justify the ways of God to men', and many people have read it as doing exactly that: praising God, attacking Satan, and laying the theology of holy scripture out in a lucid fashion. According to this reading, this is a text that represents Otherness (Satan) only to demonise it – to demonise it quite literally. Sameness, or 'cleaving to God', is Good; difference, from God, is unambiguously Bad.

What the Romantics did, though, is reread *Paradise Lost* in fertile ways. For Blake, say, Milton's epic was actually an imaginative entry into the world of difference, not sameness. Milton might claim he was writing a pious poem about God, but in fact, Blake argued, God comes out of the work as dull and uninspired, whereas Satan is a vigorous, powerfully conceived and curiously attractive character. Blake thought that this was because 'Milton was of the Devil's party without knowing it', but the unconscious motivations of the author notwithstanding, the important thing for our purposes is that, read this way, *Paradise Lost* becomes science fiction. This means more than that it concerns the exploration of an imaginatively configured solar system, or possible alien inhabitants of other worlds. *Paradise Lost* does all these things, but there are other, earlier texts that do similarly. The crucial thing is that this is a text about the most alien of aliens its author could imagine: an alien who is so radically Other than God that he cannot be contained within the universe God has created. Milton's Satan is the original bug-eyed monster.

And it is because Milton's conception of Satan is so beguiling, because, intentionally or otherwise, Milton did not simply represent Satan as an incarnation of wickedness to be easily dismissed, that *Paradise Lost* works so powerfully. And it is this aspect of the poem, this way of reading it as being about the tragic career of an overreacher, rather than being about the pious articulation of a religious ideology, as well as its imaginative recreation of Otherness in character and setting, and its mind-grabbing sense of the Sublime, that drew Romantic writers to it. It is the Romantic interest in the text that gives it a significance other classic representations of the monstrous alien, such as Grendel in the Anglo-Saxon epic *Beowulf*, do not have for the development of SF. Because, as I have argued, it is Romanticism, and more specifically the Gothic novel, that attempted to recreate the power and sublimity of Milton's hellish conception in a different setting. These attempts stand as direct forebears of modern SF.

Frankenstein, for instance, is a Gothic novel very much in dialogue with Milton. Its epigraph, quoted from Milton's poem ('Did I request thee, maker, from clay to mould me man?') suggests the ways the novel functions as a retelling of *Paradise Lost*. Frankenstein's monster even identifies himself with Milton's Satan. The monster is brought into existence and then abandoned by his creator, who was so startled by the ugliness of his creation that he literally ran away and fell into a sort of amnesiac state. Left to his own devices, the monster teaches himself to speak by overhearing the inhabitants of a remote house talking amongst themselves. He also manages, more far-fetchedly, to teach himself to read, and amongst the first books he reads is Milton's *Paradise Lost*. 'I read it,' he says, 'as a true history. It moved me to every feeling of wonder and awe' (Mary Shelley, *Frankenstein, or the Modern Prometheus* (1992): 126).

Critics sometimes express mild surprise at the range and persistence of *Frankenstein*'s influence: it continues to make its presence felt today in countless film and TV versions, as well as in texts such as James Cameron's *Terminator* (1984) that reconfigure Shelley's novel in a machine SF idiom. And it has this influence despite the fact that it is amateurishly constructed and gushingly written; one critic calls it 'an immature work which nevertheless has been enormously influential' (Parrinder 1979: 11). But the secret of *Frankenstein*'s success is not hard to divine. It is in the detailed manifestation of the beautiful strangeness of the monster that the book strikes home; it is, in other words, the way its central character, who is also its novum, functions as an embodiment of alterity. The strategies Shelley uses to this end are various. Most obviously there is the sheer novelty of the creature's origins, 'manufactured' by a scientist. In a later preface Shelley first added the suggestion that electricity may have played some part in animating the thing; in the novel as we have it there are no details as to how this feat was achieved. Along similar lines, the extremities of experience in the novel, the extreme violence, the extreme fear, are Gothic attempts at sublimity, at articulating a state of being other than the ordinary. The polar landscapes of the novel's conclusion are the apotheosis of this. The narrator encounters both Frankenstein and his 'monstrous' creation in an environment as far removed from the sorts of environment we are used to as it is possible to find on the surface of this planet. This symphony of Gothic difference produces some of the novel's most overwrought passages. Frankenstein pursues his monster over the polar ice-cap, a land that metaphorically reproduces the alienated strangeness of the novel's central conceit: 'Oh!' the narrator declares, 'how unlike it was to the blue seasons of the south!' (p. 199). Frankenstein almost apprehends him, but the elements intervene.

> But now, when I appeared almost within grasp of my foe...the wind arose; the sea roared; and, as with the mighty shock of an earthquake, it split, and cracked with a tremendous and overwhelming sound...in a few minutes a tumultuous sea rolled

between me and my enemy, and I was left drifting on a scattered piece of ice.

(Mary Shelley, *Frankenstein* (1992): 201)

This sort of writing is clumsy, maybe, but it does possess a certain gnashing vividness. A passage like this symbolically apprehends the themes of the novel, what Aldiss calls 'the disintegration of society which follows man's arrogation of power. We see one perversion of the natural order leading to another' (Aldiss 1973: 27). Shelley's novum, the alienated monster, articulates the way 'science' cuts itself off from the more organic processes of nature, and in turn functions as a symbol for a modern sense of alienated existence. Darko Suvin argues that *Frankenstein* sets in motion a recurrent theme of SF, the idea that 'progress becomes indissoluble from catastrophe' (Suvin 1979: 10).

JULES VERNE AND H G WELLS

Important though Shelley's novel has been in the development of SF, it is not until the end of the nineteenth century, and the work of Verne and Wells, that we start to see the actual growth of SF as a meaningful category in its own right, which is to say, as something more than the occasional single novel. And it is through Wells, rather than Verne, that fiction centrally concerned with the encounter with difference is most thoroughly developed.

Jules Verne (1828–1905) was particularly adept at stories of fantastic voyages. *Voyage au centre de la terre* (*Voyage to the Centre of the Earth*, 1863) follows its protagonists down the shaft of an extinct Icelandic volcano into the hollow space at the Earth's core; its narrative and descriptive evocations of the sublime give it an imaginative potency. In particular Verne's vision of enormous subterranean caverns filled with primal oceans containing dinosaur monsters functions as an effective symbol of the same unconscious arena represented by so many Gothic cellars, dungeons and caves. Other works by Verne are grounded in a particular, rationalist perspective on the virtues of technology. We see this in the much-filmed *20,000 lieues sous les mers* (*Twenty Thousand Leagues Under the Sea*, 1872), with its high-tech (for the 1870s) submarine, the 'Nautilus'; or the more obviously SF *De la terre à la lune* (*From the Earth to the Moon*, 1865), in which the protagonists' spaceship achieves escape velocity by being fired from an enormous cannon. All Verne's books are set in a version of his present day, and when he invented such SF props as a spaceship he was keen to work them from existing scientific principles. The principle of lunar exploration outlined in *De la terre à la lune* seems outlandish to us, but Verne thought it preferable to the sorts of device imagined by his contemporaries. H G Wells also wrote a story about lunar exploration: *The First Men in the Moon* (1901). In this novel, a scientist invents a metal that resists gravity, and constructs a sphere of this material inside which he and a friend are able to float off the face of the Earth and eventually to make their way to the Moon. Verne was not impressed, and commented on Wells's novel, getting the details wrong to be doubly disdainful:

> I make use of physics. He invents. I go to the moon in a cannon-ball, discharged from a cannon. Here there is no invention. He goes to Mars in an airship, which he constructs of a material which does away with the laws of gravitation. *Ca c'est très joli* [that's all very well]...but show me this metal. Let him produce it.
>
> (Verne, quoted in Parrinder 1980: 7)

The effect, in Verne's fiction, is, as John Clute puts it, 'a sense of coming very close to but never toppling over the edge of the known' (Clute and Nicholls 1993: 1276). There is, in other words, a certain limitation to the Verneian encounter with difference.

H G Wells (1866–1946) is, as the critic Patrick Parrinder has put it, 'the pivotal figure in the evolution of scientific romance into modern science fiction. His example has done as much to shape SF as any other single literary influence' (Parrinder 1980: 10). Parrinder thinks this has to do with Wells's skill in generic combination, added to the fact that he mastered a range of 'representative themes (time-travel, the alien invasion, biological mutation, the future-city, the anti-utopia)'. But behind all of this is a Wellsian fascination with encountering difference embodied in material form, and a lucid sense of the symbolic possibilities of the imaginative novum. Nearly all his early stories concern men meeting strange life forms; for instance 'The Stolen Bacillus', 'In the Avu Observatory', 'The Flowering of the Strange Orchid' and 'Aepyornis Island', all of which were published in 1894. His early short novel, *The Island of Doctor Moreau* (1896), is a powerful reworking of *Frankenstein*, and through Shelley a revisioning of Milton's *Paradise Lost*. Wells's scientist, the vivisectionist Moreau, has sequestered himself on a tropical island, where he has been surgically reworking various animals, making their physiques more human and enhancing their brains. These creations are 'monstrous' in much the way that Shelley's monster was; which is to say, they are both repulsive and also oddly attractive, beautifully strange. They have developed a primitive religion, centred on Moreau as a combined God of Mercy and Pain; as they chant: '*His* is the Hand that wounds, *His* is the Hand that heals'. The novel's Gothic Eden also includes a version of the Biblical 'Tree of the Knowledge of Good and Evil' in Moreau's injunction to the beast-men not to taste blood . This command is, of course, transgressed, and the beast-men revert to their bestial origins. All this provides Wells with a straightforward vehicle for satirising religion. But it is the variety of beast-men themselves, based on dogs, pumas, pigs, monkeys – 'they wore turbans too, and thereunder peered out their elfin faces at me, faces with protruding lower jaws and bright eyes' (Wells, *The Science Fiction, Vol. 1*

(1995): 96) – and others that stick in the imagination. As a novum they enable Wells to write fluently about the balance between civilisation and bestiality in humankind. Aldiss considers William Golding's *Lord of the Flies* and George Orwell's *Animal Farm* to be 'this novel's descendants' (Aldiss 1973: 122), but the advantage in embodying the story in a science-fictional idiom is that the connection between bestialism and humanity is established in the logic of the text via exactly the discourse of scientific rationalism that the novel goes on to deconstruct, rather than conceptualising it in naturalistic terms, like Golding, or as fable like Orwell.

Wells's most famous novel of the encounter with difference – indeed, one of the most famous SF novels of all – is *The War of the Worlds* (1898). One of the reasons this novel has had such a lasting impact on the traditions of science fiction has to do with the way Wells is able to work his material into a sort of wrought, mournful beauty something akin to poetry. He takes a perfectly ordinary man, an especially ordinary place, Woking, and then he imagines the extraordinary erupting into it, in the form of a giant cylinder crashing to Earth from Mars. Tentacled Martians climb out of this cylinder to make war upon humanity from towering mechanical tripods, laying waste to South East England before eventually succumbing to Earthly bacteria against which they have no natural defence. But all this is rendered that much more effective by Wells's impeccable sense of the interlinked beauties of the familiar and the strange. The early chapters of the book build an understated but brilliant sense of anticipation by stressing that very ordinariness.

> There were lights in the upper windows of the houses as the people went to bed. From the railway station in the distance came the sound of shunting trains, ringing and rumbling, softened almost to melody by the distance...It seemed so safe and tranquil.
>
> (Wells, *The Science Fiction, Vol. 1* (1995): 189)

The same sort of poetry that Wells can find in the evening shunt-
ings of trains at Woking is repeated in the desolate beauty he
evokes in a London emptied by the Martian threat and overrun
with the red weed they have brought across space. At this point
in the book the last Martian is ceasing its weird cry and dying.

> Abruptly as I crossed the bridge, the sound of 'Ulla, ulla, ulla,
> ulla' ceased. It was, as it were, cut off. The silence came like a
> thunder-clap.
>
> The dusky houses about me stood faint and tall and dim;
> the trees towards the park were growing black. All about me
> the red weed clambered among the ruins, writhing to get
> above me in the dimness. Night, the mother of fear and mys-
> tery, was coming upon me. But while that voice sounded the
> solitude, the desolation, had been endurable; by virtue of it,
> London had still seemed alive, and the sense of life about me
> had upheld me. Then suddenly a change, the passing of some-
> thing – I knew not what – and then a stillness that could be
> felt.
>
> (Wells, *The Science Fiction, Vol. 1* (1995): 309–10)

It is less the specifics of finding a beautiful strangeness in this
scenario, and more the ways in which it parallels the scenes of
calm before the war; it is Wells's dialectical sense of the interrela-
tionship between sameness and otherness that gives this work
much of its potency: the cognitive estrangement, in other words.

Wells's potently imagined nova in *The War of the Worlds* symbolically distil the concerns of the age. His Martians are imperial-
ists who use their superior technology to invade a nation,
England, which had been accumulating its own Empire in part
because of a superior technological sophistication. In other words,
the arrival of the Martians and their mechanised brutalities are
the symbolic forms Wells chose to explore a deeper set of concerns: concerns about the British (rather than the Martian)

Empire, about the violence of Empire-building, and about the anxieties of otherness and the encounter with otherness that Empire imposes on the Imperial peoples. Aldiss suggests that Wells's novel 'showed the Imperialist European powers of the day how it felt to be on the receiving end of an invasion armed with superior technology' (Aldiss 1973: 71), but in fact the text is not as straightforwardly turn-about as that. Wells actually inhabits a subtly balanced position between expressing concern about the morality of European Imperialism in coded form, and reinforcing exactly the ideological underpinnings of that Imperialism with a scare story about how easily a ruthless, racially distinct military threat might destroy an underprepared Britain. More specifically, there is something 'Eastern' about Wells's conception of his Martians, from their pseudo-Arabic cry of 'Ulla', like the Islamic cry of 'Allah', to their towering mechanical tripods striding about on metal legs which may derive from Russian folklore of a house that moves about on gigantic chicken legs. In other words, the deftness of Wells's conception is that he is able simultaneously to critique the European Imperial excesses, whilst also coding the 'Eastern' threat against which European Imperialism specifically justified itself. Suvin captures something of this ideological ambiguity by invoking the name of Nazi propagandist and anti-Semite Joseph Goebbels.

> The Martians from *The War of the Worlds* are described in Goebbelsian terms of repugnantly slimy and horrible 'racial' otherness and given the sole function of bloodthirsty predators (a function that fuses genocidal fire-power – itself described as an echo of the treatment meted out by the imperialist powers to colonized peoples – with the bloodsucking vampirism of horror fantasies).
>
> (Suvin 1979: 78)

The effectiveness of a novel like *The War of the Worlds*, in other words, depends partly upon the sophistication of its balancing of familiar representation and the strangeness of its novum; but that novum also relates symbolically back to key concerns of the society and culture out of which it was produced. It is not a narrow mapping of Imperialist anxieties onto a symbolic form, but rather a complex symbolic meditation of the paradoxes of Imperialist ideology.

Following on from this we can argue that SF as a distinctive genre comes out of the Age of Empires precisely because it is a necessary part of the official ideology of Empire-forming that difference needs to be flattened, or even eradicated. SF, in other words, figures as the expression of the subconscious aspect of this official ideology. Under the nineteenth-century British Empire the pressure is to conform upwards to a certain model of 'civilised' behaviour. We can see something similar today, under what can more loosely be called the twentieth-century American Empire, where culture treats everybody in the world, whatever their actual identity, as a 'sort-of American'. A film such as *Independence Day* (1997), for instance, figures a world catastrophe as an American catastrophe, with other nations represented in cameo as acquiescing under American leadership and sharing American values. The world, in that film, is America. Similarly, *Star Trek* postulates a 'Federation of Planets' encompassing a wide range of alien worlds, but none the less manages to flatten difference into a kind of Galactic Americana. The 'USS' in USS *Enterprise* stands for 'United Space Ship', but by no coincidence it is also the present-day abbreviation for 'United States Ship'. It is not just a question of American actors filling almost every role (which, of course, we might expect in a show filmed in Los Angeles); but of a representative cultural identity which is Western, bourgeois, family-centred, aspirational, rational, centrally concerned with 'freedom' as the freedom of individualist enterprise – American, in short. I like *Star Trek* a great deal, but its success as a series depends, it seems to me, on the ways in which it is subtly able to undercut the conformist ideological message that it tends to share with other world-winning American cultural productions. A scene in Nicholas Meyer's film *Star Trek 6: the Undiscovered Country* (1991), where the Klingons quote Shakespeare 'in the original Klingon', is an example of this: it wittily forces us to rethink our assumptions about the 'Western' cultural dominance. In the film the Klingons criticise the Federation as 'a humans-only club', foregrounding the cultural essentialism behind much of the original series.

One of the ways, then, in which an Empire establishes itself, justifies itself and continues, is by putting out the cultural message that the dominant culture in that Empire is best, and that (therefore) other cultures should conform to it. It does that on the one hand by raising up the values of the dominant culture, and on the other by attacking those who are not part of that culture. In other words it is involved in praising the Same and demonising the Other. That Other might be many things: history has given us the Other as Jew, as Black, as Arab, as East Asian ('the Yellow Peril'), and as Woman. On the other hand, history's verdict on the Same has been remarkably consistent: the Same has tended to be male, white, Western, and associated with military power and technology.

This is, it goes without saying, a crude and brief account of a complex set of cultural and historical circumstances. But my point is that science fiction first emerges as the underside to this set of cultural dominants; as, in a sense, the dark subconscious to the thinking mind of Imperialism. Where much mainstream Victorian culture, for instance, is about the patent rightness and decency of 'civilisation' as it was then conceived, science fiction explores the problematics of that term. According to this sort of model, much science fiction can be keyed into cultural and historical specifics. It is no coincidence, the argument would go, that British science fiction experienced a burst of inventive creativity at around the time of Wells, Bram Stoker (1847–1912),

Olaf Stapleton (1886–1950) and Rider Haggard (1856–1925); because this period saw the high summer of the British Imperial adventure. Similarly, the rise to world domination of the USA after the Second World War saw a cognate flourishing in American SF, the so-called 'Golden Age' of Science Fiction, leading through the 1950s and 1960s both to SF texts that articulated Imperial anxiety (for instance, *Invasion of the Body Snatchers*, 1956) but also to works (such as the ongoing *Star Trek* series) that are all about exploring the new frontier, transferring the colonisation of the American continent directly onto the galaxy.

PULP SF

Both Verne and Wells were writing deliberately popular fiction, and working within the traditions of popular publishing of their day; so it is that Wells's writing grew out of his speculative, mass-market journalism; whilst Verne struck up a lucrative deal with a publisher called Jules Hetzel, who marketed the novels under the popularising rubric of 'Voyages extraordinaires'. In America, the popular market also dictated the beginnings of SF as a serious genre.

In particular, this is connected with the cheap magazine format known as 'Pulp'. Advances in the manufacture of paper out of wood-pulp in the 1880s fuelled a boom in cheap publishing, and a wide range of magazines grew up, printed on a cheap, thick paper that shreds easily and yellows quickly. These soon began catering for specific markets, such as westerns, detective fiction and romantic love-stories. The first Pulp to specialise in what we might think of as SF was *Thrill Book*, which started publishing in 1919 and went out of business the same year. The first magazine with any commercial durability was *Amazing Stories*, which began publication in 1926. *Amazing* was founded by Luxembourg-born Hugo Gernsback, who worked hard to define the nascent field of

SF. In an editorial from 1929, Gernsback talked ambitiously about the term he also claimed to have invented.

> Not only is science fiction an idea of tremendous import, but it is to be an important factor in making the world a better place to live in, through educating the public to the possibilities of science and the influence of science on life...If every man, woman, boy and girl, could be induced to read science fiction right along, there would certainly be a great resulting benefit to the community...Science fiction would make people happier, give them a broader understanding of the world, make them more tolerant.
>
> (Gernsback, quoted in James 1994: 8–9)

Gernsback used his editorial power to shape the development of the genre, with a strong preference for SF that was grounded thoroughly in science, that was 'educational' almost to the point of being openly didactic. John Campbell, the other great name from SF magazine editorship (he took over the rival publication *Astounding Science-Fiction* in 1937), shared this belief that SF should educate as it entertained, and that it should be grounded in science and the celebration of science. At the same time, Campbell insisted of all his contributors that the science should be properly integrated into the story, that there should be no undigested scientific lectures dropped into the text. More than Gernsback, Campbell believed that SF should be about more than just machines and ideas, that the focus should rather be on the ways people responded to and were shaped by those ideas.

However noble these ideas sound, it cannot be denied that the 'Pulps' have a reputation for a very different sort of fiction: for kinetic, fast-paced and exciting tales that are also clumsily written, hurried in conception, and morally crude. The critics Clute and Nicholls cite a nicely representative blurb from a 1931 edition of *Astounding*, concerning a story entitled 'The Pirate Planet' by Charles W Diffin: 'From Earth & Sub-Venus Converge a Titanic Offensive of Justice on the Unspeakable Man-Things of Torg' (Clute and Nicholls 1993: 63). Unspeakable Man-Things – demonisations of otherness, in other words – and their analogues also characterised the look of the Pulps; their brightly-coloured, crudely realised cover art was as much part of the effect of the text as the writing inside, representing, for example, men in spacesuits and women in less complete clothing being menaced by insectoid, ape-like or otherwise monstrous aliens. As the critic Edward James puts it, 'the American Pulps may have bequeathed a largely unfortunate heritage to SF in the second half of the twentieth century'. James deplores 'their concentration on action not thought, on power rather than responsibility, on aggression not introspection, on wish fulfillment not reality', and goes on to quote Thomas Disch's mournful judgement from his article 'The Embarrassments of Science Fiction', that 'by far the great part of pulp fiction from the time of Wells till now was written to provide a semi-literate audience with compensatory fantasies' (James 1994: 48).

One of the less-defensible aspects of this was the repeated use of a Wellsian trope of alien invasion in order to celebrate the superiority of humankind over the unprovoked threat from an unspeakable alien menace. This is evident in works such as Edgar Rice Burroughs's *The Moon Maid* (1926) or the comic-strip *Buck Rogers in the 25th Century*, which first appeared in 1929, and which was based by Philip Nowlan on his novel *Armageddon 2419*, which in turn had appeared in *Amazing* during 1928–9. In the original incarnation of this adventure Buck Rogers, sent 500 years into the future, discovers that America has been overrun by the evil hordes of 'Red Mongols', and immediately sets-to to battle against the menace. One of the imitators of this successful strip, *Flash Gordon* (which first appeared as a comic strip in 1934), makes the anti-orientalism of the concept more explicit, with its Chinese-style villain, the embodiment of all that is evil, the Emperor Ming the Merciless of the Planet Mongo. This coding of invasion paranoia was sometimes even more direct: Heinlein's 1941 novel *Sixth Column*, which first appeared in *Astounding*, is specifically about an Asian invasion of the USA. In each of these cases, SF is being used to reinforce a particular, narrow ideological construction of 'American-ness' by demonising some notional scapegoat.

But sometimes the energy and sprawling inventiveness of the Pulps produced more interesting, viable SF. Two authors particularly associated with the Pulps have endured, partly because they were able to fashion something lastingly strange from the materials of the rapidly solidifying genre in which they worked. Edgar Rice Burroughs (1875–1950) was a prolific and inventive writer, who is probably best remembered today for inventing Tarzan, Lord of the Jungle. More relevant, for our purposes, is his sequence of eleven Mars novels, sometimes called the *Barsoom* sequence, after the name the natives of Mars give their own planet. The first of these, *A Princess of Mars*, first appeared as early as 1912, in *All-Story Magazine*; but Burroughs was still writing them in the 1940s. His hero is as all-American as Buck Rogers or Flash Gordon, although there is an element of myth, or even mysticism, in Burroughs's conception that tends to unravel the harder-edged SF aspects. Carter, a warrior, does not travel to Mars in a spaceship, but effectively by praying to his 'god', Mars, and finding himself simply transported there. Once there he battles against aliens with many arms and various coloured skins (blue, black, green); but he also marries a Martian Princess who is beautiful despite being – or, arguably, *because* she is – red-skinned and egg-laying. It is hard to deny the racism and sexism that underlie much of Burroughs's works of fiction, but there is also enough which is strange in them to unsettle the fixed notions of that sort of bigotry. Most of the fighting is with swords, even though there are various nova on Barsoom that are more advanced, such as radium pistols and antigravity fliers. As we saw with *Dune*, the

combination of technological advance and retro-styled old-fashionedness focuses the nostalgic cast of the mode. Burroughs's
Barsoom is a backward-looking civilisation, a world that is dying
with a decaying population and drying oceans; its various nova in
fact externalise an American perspective on the East not dissimi-
lar to the cruder, morally coloured demonisations of the orient
mentioned above. Aldiss quotes a passage from A *Princess of Mars*
in which Carter joins a caravan of green-skinned aliens travelling
across a dried Martian seabed.

> We made a most imposing, an awe-inspiring spectacle as we
> strung out across the yellow landscape; the two hundred and
> fifty ornate and brightly coloured chariots, preceded by an
> advance guard of some two hundred mounted warriors...The
> gleaming metals and jewels of the men and women, dupli-
> cated in the trappings of the zitidars and thoats [Martian ani-
> mals], and interspersed with the flashing colours of
> magnificent silks and furs and feathers, lent a barbaric splen-
> dour to the caravan which would have turned an East Indian
> potentate green with envy.

As Aldiss observes, 'to speak of turning potentates green gives
the game away, for this is clearly what he is doing, transposing an
Eastern sumptuousness to Mars' (Aldiss 1973: 160–1). Just as
telling is the adjective 'barbaric', with its overtones of anti-
orientalist ideological reductiveness. But despite the problematics
of Burroughs's texts, their imaginative power has swept up several generations of readers. Edward James, for instance, confesses
to finding it hard to resist 'riding in [his] imagination on a six-
legged thoat across Barsoom's dry sea-beds, underneath its
hurtling moons, and alongside John Carter' (James 1994: 46).

E E 'Doc' Smith (1890–1965) was an equally prolific Pulp
author. It is symptomatic of Gernsback's attempts to dignify the
newly coined 'science fiction' with scientific respectability that he

insisted on adding 'PhD' to Smith's name for his contributions to *Amazing*: in fact, Smith had earned his doctorate for his contributions to food science, and specialised in doughnut batter. But the *Lensman* novels for which Smith is most famous are distinguished less by a Gernsbackian adherence to the protocols of science and more by a muscular and colourful imaginative fictionalising, a Scholesian 'fabulation'. Effectively, he invented that sub-genre known as 'Space Opera'. Smith shares with Burroughs a fundamental 'good versus evil' vision of the universe in the *Lensman* books, beginning with *Triplanetary* in 1934 and including half a dozen titles that picture a universe divided between the alien embodiments of Good, the Arisians, and the epitomes of Evil, the Eddorians. In terms of the representation of difference, this is not a conception that allows for much subtlety. The Arisians are humanoid, but the Eddorians are shaped as revoltingly different to mankind.

> Arisia was Earth-like...Eddore was and is large and dense; its liquid a poisonous, sludgy syrup; its atmosphere a foul and corrosive fog...Each Eddorian changed, not only its shape, but also its texture, in accordance with the requirements of the moment. Each produced – extruded – members whenever it needed them...filaments or cables; fingers or feet; needles or mauls.
>
> (Smith, *Triplanetary* (1997): 2–4)

These dubious shape-shifting aliens operate behind the scenes of the galaxy, hidden but manipulating it towards its doom. The Arisians, on the other hand, have been breeding human beings to the stage that, with the series protagonist Kim Kinnison, they can take on the minions of the Eddorians and defeat them. The Eddorians, in addition to being physically repulsive and morally evil, are utterly single-minded. In place of the diversity that is central to Smith's notion of 'Civilisation', 'each and every

Eddorian' had only one goal: 'power. *Power*! P-O-W-E-R!!' (p. 5). This does not represent a particularly high level of analysis.

Where Smith's novels manage to overcome these limitations is in the sheer size and scope of his imaginative conception. It is hard to think of any SF novels as enamoured of enormity as the *Lensman* books, or of Smith's other major sequence of novels, the *Skylark* series. Spaceships are enormous, and become more and more vast as Smith's career progresses. There may be a certain quaintness about the description in earlier novels: the *Fearless*, for instance, 'the British super-dreadnought, which was to be the flagship of the fleet – the mightiest and heaviest spaceship which had yet lifted her stupendous mass into the ether' (*Triplanetary*, p. 171). But when reading through Smith's novels in sequence, the proliferation of superlatives of size – 'enormous', 'vast', 'awful', 'colossal', 'mighty', 'stupendous', 'immense' and so on – does batter one's reading sensibilities into a sort of apprehension of awe, an approximation of Miltonic sublimity in an SF idiom. Smith's imaginative conception crosses huge stretches of time and space, and deploys monumental artefacts. He originally conceived the *Lensman* books as one suitably titanic single novel, 400,000 words in length. Only in the immensity of space, it could be argued, would Smith be able to find a proper correlative for the ambition of his imaginative conception.

More than this, there is a narrative principle of revealing greater and greater perspectives, of the gradual unveiling of a more and more high-reaching hierarchy, that is absolutely key to the effect of Smith's novels. I started my brief account of the novels with the description of the Arisians and the Eddorians which is found at the beginning of the (chronologically) earliest of his books. But the human protagonists have no idea that these two ancient alien races are orchestrating things behind the scenes. Smith's character Kinnison works his way up the universal hierarchy, from Earthly, the Galactic Patrol, which is a group distantly sponsored by the Arisians to fight evil, to the Lensmen, certain select members of the patrol who are allowed to wear the 'Lens', a bracelet which enhances telepathic powers, and so on upwards. As John Clute puts it, 'Kinnison never knows that the layer just penetrated has layers behind it, and has never so much as heard of the Eddorians; each new volume of the sequence, therefore, begins with the revelation that the Universe is greater, and requires greater powers to confront, than Kinnison has hitherto imagined.' Clute thinks that 'it was almost certainly these *controlled* jumps in scale that fascinated most early readers of the series' (Clute and Nicholls 1993: 1124). This technique had become another staple of SF; a TV series such as *The X-Files* has tantalised its audience over its numerous series with a very similarly orchestrated set of revelatory shifts, by which at first the government is represented as being behind the mysteries of the show, then a shadowy organisation above the government, and finally the malign space-aliens themselves.

Behind this commitment to an aesthetic of scale is a form of elitism that justifies the fan in the belief that SF is a superior genre to conventional literatures precisely because it encompasses grander and more significant vistas. Smith himself, in 1940, asserted that

> The casual reader does not understand science fiction, does not have sufficient imagination or depth or breadth of vision to grasp it, and hence does not like it...We science [fiction fans] are imaginative, with a tempered, analytical imaginativeness which fairy tales will not satisfy. We are critical. We are fastidious. We have a mental grasp and scope.
>
> (Smith, quoted in Huntington 1989: 48)

This amounts to a definition of SF similar to that of Darko Suvin or Robert Scholes, as blending 'imaginative fabulation' and 'cognitive rigour'; but the unashamed rhetoric of superiority makes clear that the novum of cosmic scale does nothing less than map onto a belief in the cognate scale and range of the SF fan's mental faculties.

THE GOLDEN AGE: ASIMOV

There was, then, a great deal of bad SF produced in America before the Second World War; but at the same time occasional successes, and, more importantly, a framework was laid in which the representation of a radical alterity could be undertaken. As American fortunes grew, this especially American mode of literature took on some of the energy and ebullience of its national outlook.

According to James, 'during the 1940s and 1950s American SF developed in maturity and complexity, and above all in sheer quantity' (James 1994: 54). Fans talk unironically of 'the Golden Age' in SF, and they usually mean something quite specific: the late 1930s and early 1940s, or sometimes, even more specifically, American Pulp publishing in the period 1938–46. This is a short period of time, but it includes a striking wealth and diversity of writing talents: Isaac Asimov, Clifford Simak, Jack Williamson, L Sprague De Camp, Theodore Sturgeon, Robert Heinlein and A E Van Vogt, to name only the shortest list that might be drawn up. The energy and self-confidence of practitioners and fans of SF during this period were extraordinary. In 1948, Joseph Campbell, the editor of the SF magazine *Astounding*, who according to Edward James 'helped to create modern SF', could talk about SF as something larger than literature.

> That group of writings which is usually referred to as 'mainstream literature' is actually a special subgroup of the field of science fiction – for science fiction deals with all places in the Universe, and all times in Eternity, so the literature of the here-and-now is, truly, a subset of science fiction.
>
> (Campbell, quoted in James 1994: 57)

The rhetoric, which resembles the Smith quotation at the end of the previous section in its expansive optimism about the inherent value of the form, is symbolically Imperial in so far as it sees SF colonising the entire territory of literature, making the mainstream a subsidiary kingdom.

To concentrate on one of the names from this Golden Age, Isaac Asimov, is to draw out the parallels between Golden Age writing and the Pulp writing that preceded it. To many, it would be a sort of critical sacrilege to suggest that E E 'Doc' Smith, popular though he is, can be equated with Isaac Asimov. Smith was a hack SF writer who managed some fairly impressive effects, whereas, in the words of C N Manlove, 'for many readers of science fiction, Isaac Asimov is the presiding genius of the genre, the old master who revolutionised the form and provided the basis for many of its present characteristics' (Manlove 1986: 15). None the less, in a work such as Asimov's highly regarded and much-imitated *Foundation* series, we see a fundamentally Smithesque imaginative process at work.

Asimov's *Foundation* books are set at the close of a Galactic Empire. A scientist – or 'psychohistorian' as Asimov terms it – called Hari Seldon has analysed with mathematical exactness the way that history works. He can, according to Asimov's conception, do this for the history of a million people to the extent of precisely anticipating the future, although with individuals there are too many variables to enable him to do this. He foresees the downfall of the Empire and the ten thousand years of chaos that will follow. So he sets up his Foundation, ostensibly a group which is compiling the *Encyclopedia Galactica* but which is actually working to preserve and rebuild civilisation, in order to bring society back to normal in a tenth of the time. The novels chart the exact success of Sheldon's prophesies, until a mutant individual called 'the Mule' (so-called because he is sterile) is born. Sheldon could predict the mass dynamics of society, but had no way of knowing what freak individuals might arise. As it is, the Mule smashes the Foundation's carefully constructed new civilisation in a drive for power, and is only stopped by a mysterious 'Second Foundation' established by Sheldon to step into the breach should the First Foundation fail.

The Mule is the only random element in Asimov's conception of the future, and even that dramatic device was pressed on him by John Campbell. There is something almost comforting in the central conception, though: that history itself may be completely comprehended and therefore controlled. In terms of the encounter with difference, this is the flaw in the work. It transpires that nothing unexpected can happen in Asimov's universe: even the unexpected – the Mule – was expected after all, and Sheldon had prepared for its eventuality with a secretive, hidden organisation, the so-called Second Foundation. Indeed, where at the beginning of the work we assume that Sheldon's plan was simply to ease humankind over the break-up of the Galactic Empire, by the time the Second Foundation is revealed we realise that his conception was grander: to put an end to historical flux altogether. That there is a slightly sinister edge to this seems difficult to doubt; not only that these novels set themselves at loggerheads with the randomness of diversity, but that they embody within themselves precisely that aesthetic of the Same. Colin Manlove talks about the controlled aesthetic monotony of the conception of these novels: 'persons are usually seen as typical rather than special, even as clichés…we do not know how one planet differs from another…nor are we given details of battles, lingering accounts of love, different customs of civilisations. There are no animals, only man…Thought-processes and conversations largely fill the trilogy, and nearly all these are confined to finding things out and with gaining power' (Manlove 1986: 28–9).

Frank Herbert's *Dune* novels are often seen as an attempt to rewrite Asimov's great epic in terms that might take account of the necessary randomness of historical process; to reconfigure them, in other words, so as to take more account of difference.

There's an elitism behind Asimov's novels that grates. Indeed, Herbert has commented upon Asimov's *Foundation* books in exactly these terms.

> History [in the *Foundation* books]...is manipulated for larger ends and for the greater good as determined by scientific aristocracy. It is assumed, then, that the scientist-shamans know best what course humankind should take...While surprises may appear in these stories (e.g. the Mule mutant), it is assumed that no surprise will be too great or too unexpected to overcome the firm grasp of science upon human destiny. This is essentially the assumption that science can produce a surprise-free future for humankind.
>
> (Herbert, quoted in OReilly 1981: 87)

At the same time, it is worth stressing – lest my account here should seem too harsh – the excitement with which many readers respond to the power of Asimov's imaginative conception. Even critics with negative comments on the books concede their effectiveness; Manlove, whom I have quoted at length, calls it 'this brilliant work'. That has a great deal to do with the scale and range of Asimov's imagination; to produce a novel of ideas, a novel that philosophically engages with questions of historiography (which is to say, the nature and theory of history, the way history works) and epistemology (questions of knowledge and the ways in which it is possible to know anything), and that does so on the largest possible scales of space and time, really does sweep the reader along. And in the sense that this novel approaches the sort of sublimity associated with vastness, Asimov is working the same aesthetic line as E E 'Doc' Smith. Like Smith, he stages his psychohistory via a series of dramatically effective unveilings of deeper truths, more hidden mysteries. The Foundation organisation itself is hidden behind the façade of a group compiling the *Encyclopedia Galactica*, and only reveals itself during the course of the first novel. With the reversals of the Mule, Asimov pulls away another curtain to reveal the Second Foundation. By the time we have moved through several books in the sequence, to *Foundation's Edge* (1982), Asimov has revealed an even deeper truth: that the universe itself in its present form owes its existence to an ancient race of Eternals who chose from a plethora of possibilities the universe we now inhabit, in which man is the only sentient life form. A greater plan, similarly deterministic, underlies his character Seldon's conception of history as something to be controlled.

This aesthetic of scale is more sophisticated in its workings-out than in the Pulp writing of the 1920s and 1930s, but it relates symbolically to the same ideological concerns. As John Huntington argues:

> At the core of much SF fantasy is an identification with power. We see it in recent SF by an exaltation in sheer size: empires war with ships the size of planets. A student once explained to me that SF was interesting and important because the weapons it imagined were capable of destroying a planet, even a universe. How trivial the cowboy's six-shooter was by comparison. Such an observation is not entirely naïve.
>
> (Huntington 1989: 44)

NEW WAVE

If 'Golden Age' SF mirrors the bullishness of the American experience of the 1940s, there are many examples of 1950s SF that mirror an increasing unease. From Asimov's confidence that science, applied properly, could solve all problems, we find in the 1950s an increasing scepticism. During the later 1950s, American society was convulsed with a paranoid campaign against communism lead by Senator Joe McCarthy: people were publicly condemned for not embracing 'American values' with enough zeal. McCarthy believed that agents from the old Soviet Union were infiltrating American society, and turning, as he saw it, 'good' American citizens into secret 'evil' communists. This climate of political paranoia, with its fearful conformity and obsessive focusing on the Alien as Enemy, fed directly through into SF imaginations. Jack Finney wrote a novel called *Body Snatchers* in 1955, in which a small American town is invaded by alien spores from space that grow into exact copies of individual human beings whilst destroying their originals. This was made into a highly regarded film in 1956, *Invasion of the Body Snatchers*, directed by Don Siegel. The effectiveness of both texts depends to a large extent on how finely balanced they are as political satire. Indeed they can be read *both* as right-wing McCarthyite scare-mongering – Communists from an Alien place are infiltrating our American towns and wiping out their American values, and the worst of it is *they look exactly like Americans* – and as left-wing liberal satire on the ideological climate of conformism that McCarthyism produced, where the lack of emotion of the pod-people corresponds to the ethical blind eyes turned by Americans to the persecutions of their fellows by over-zealous McCarthyites.

Critics are divided as to exactly when SF stopped being a minority interest and became a mass phenomenon. According to Edward James it was during the 1950s that SF experienced a 'boom in America' which led to an explosive 'growth in SF readership'. James thinks that this readership was 'inspired perhaps by worries about the future (for the cold war fostered paranoia of all kinds)' (James 1994: 84). According to John Huntington, on the other hand, it was not until the 1960s and what is called 'New Wave SF' that the genre became a genuinely mass, popular phenomenon. It is certainly the case that during the sixties a number of 'cult' novels achieved enormous international popularity, starting with devoted fans on university campuses and spreading out. Three such texts are Tolkien's *The Lord of the Rings* (1954–55; as Fantasy, this work is outside the range of a study of

SF), Heinlein's massive *Stranger in a Strange Land* (1961) and Herbert's *Dune* (1965). According to Huntington (1989), 'by the sixties SF had crossed a boundary and ceased to be the literature of only an intensely devoted minority'. The broad popularity in the late sixties of *Stranger in a Strange Land* and *Dune* is a phenomenon quite unlike the comparatively select popularity of 'Golden Age SF'. Huntington explicitly links this burgeoning popularity with the shifting ideological tenor of the times:

> The growth of new wave SF in the sixties can be seen as a rendering of attitudes implicit in the SF of the middle and late fifties. It is not accidental that the flourishing of the new wave in SF coincides with a decade of political activism and of skepticism about technological solutions to social and environmental problems.
>
> (Huntington 1989: 2)

There was also a shift in the economic dynamics of publishing during the 1950s and 1960s. Where magazine publishing had been the norm throughout the 1940s, in the 1950s the balance shifted towards books. Publishers woke up particularly to the possibilities of paperback production, and by the 1960s magazines were experiencing a gradual decline in circulation numbers, whilst more and more novels were being published. A number of writers began working out their ideas at novel length, rather than 'fixing up' novels from previously published shorter pieces. And much of the (arguably) ideologically monolithic writing of the Golden Age became subject to critique: its underlying assumptions about culture and society were challenged. In place of a rationalist belief in the effectiveness of technology and machinery to solve all human problems, there came an avant-garde 'experimental literature' fascination with the artistic possibilities of those very problems, and in particular a paranoid aesthetic in which all large systems were seen as the enemies of individual difference. Philip K Dick, who remains one of the most highly regarded of all SF writers, is the classic embodiment of this New Wave aesthetic; I will discuss briefly Dick's distinctive paranoid aesthetic in Chapter 5.

The scale and ambition of *Dune* have been mentioned at the end of Chapter 1; they owe much to the effects of scale found in Pulp and Golden Age SF, although Herbert deploys them for different reasons. In part, this is because the mystical agenda of the novel, combined with its abandonment of technological nova, marks *Dune* very much as a product of the countercultural environment of the 1960s; something enhanced by the ubiquity of the drug 'Spice' to Herbert's imagined world. A work like Heinlein's *Stranger in a Strange Land* seems today even more obviously rooted in the 'drop-out' hippy counterculture of its time. Some critics have expressed surprise that a book by so right-wing, libertarian and gun-obsessed a writer as Heinlein should have achieved cult status amongst university students and hippies. But *Stranger in a Strange Land* lengthily and deliberately adopts the perspective of difference that identified it easily with the countercultural beliefs of many of its readers. Its central character, Valentine Michael Smith, has an outsider's perspective of Earth, being born on Mars and raised by Martians. His adventures on our planet allow him to act as spokesman for a number of anti-status-quo positions; his own philosophy is founded on the idea of 'grokking', a word Heinlein coined which has now become part of the English language (to 'grok' means to establish a rapport with, to empathise with someone intuitively, something the telepathic Smith can manage easily). In the novel, this becomes the foundation for a defence of free love. 'Sex,' says one of the characters elaborating the Michael Smith gospel, '*should* be a means of happiness.'

> The code says 'thou shalt not covet thy neighbour's wife.' The result? Reluctant chastity, adultery, jealousy, bitterness, blows

and sometimes murder, broken homes and twisted children –
and furtive little passes degrading to woman and man. Is this
commandment ever obeyed?...

Now comes [Valentine Michael Smith] and says: 'there is no
need to covet my wife...love her! There's no limit to her love,
we have everything to gain – and nothing to lose but fear and
guilt and hatred and jealousy.' This proposition is incredible.

(Heinlein, *Stranger in a Strange Land* (1993): 432)

For a culture fascinated with difference and diversity, Smith
becomes an iconic messiah figure. The blend of hedonism and
mysticism represented in the book captures exactly how the
science-fictional point of difference can become the platform for a
cultural movement that specifically defines itself as different from
mainstream culture. At the same time, as Aldiss points out,
Heinlein's book is also the straightforward inheritor of a 'well
established and respectable pulp tradition of the all-powerful
male, so largely epitomised in John W. Campbell's swaggering
intergalactic heroes' (Aldiss 1973: 274).

At the close of this brief survey chapter, there are two further
things worth stressing about SF from the 1960s to the present
day. One is that the challenges to the totalising assumptions of
'Golden Age' SF manifested themselves in more fundamental
ways than just the subject matter of the texts themselves. Every
single twentieth-century author I have mentioned in this chapter
so far has been white and male. One of the most significant
aspects of the development of the genre has been the growth of
authors of colour; another is the rise of women authors of SF, so
much so that it is probably fair to say that the present-day giants
of the field are Ursula Le Guin and Octavia Butler. But even
more significant than this eruption of alterity into the structures
of production of SF itself is the enormous growth in popularity of
the genre. Partly this has been novel-led; with certain authors
and certain texts (I have already mentioned Heinlein and

Herbert) achieving first cult and then international success. But a more significant factor, in terms of the sheer numbers of people attracted to SF, has been TV and cinema. First came the success of *Star Trek*, which was, in truth, a slightly belated success. Paramount made three series of the show (1966–8) and then cancelled it, following only modest ratings; but a dedicated fan-base and a growing audience created by re-runs through the 1970s eventually turned *Trek* into the most successful televisual SF phenomenon. By the mid-1970s the climate was right for a single cinema film, *Star Wars* (1977), to ignite an astonishing popular engagement with SF. It is due to *Star Wars* that the cinematic climate of Hollywood shifted so thoroughly towards SF, and that (as a result) over half of the top-grossing films of all time are science-fictional (the four *Star Wars* films, *ET*, *Jurassic Park*, the *Terminator* films, the *Alien* sequence and *Independence Day* have all made hundreds of millions of dollars).

A more detailed examination of post-1960s SF takes place in the next three chapters, which look at the rise of women's SF, and at questions of race and of technology in the genre. But I want to finish this chapter by looking at a text that exhibits this recursive tendency of SF, which is to say, the way in which SF texts today make use of and refer back to the very history of the genre I have been sketching in this chapter. A film such as *Star Wars* exists in very close relationship with the conventions and strengths of Pulp and Golden Age SF.

CASE STUDY: *STAR WARS* (1977) AND INTERTEXTUALITY

It was *Star Wars* that jump-started SF in the 1970s, turning it from a vigorous but fairly small-scale genre into the dominant mode of cinematic discourse. It is a crucial text for any study of post war SF, not only because of its astonishing success and the vitality of the fan-culture which has grown up around it, but because it marks a sort of way-station in the literary traditions of the genre. *Star Wars* mediates the Pulp SF heritage of the Golden Age, and translates it into something larger-scale, bigger-budget, more sophisticated and glossy.

One of the joys of *Star Wars* is precisely the way it straddles the traditions of SF, the homely virtues of melodrama and adventure that we associate with Pulp SF on the one hand, and the techno-sophisticated brilliance of 1980s special-effects SF on the other. It looks back and it looks forward. In fact it is the backward-looking aspects of the film that are dominant. So it is no coincidence that this film begins with the legend 'A Long Time Ago, in a Galaxy Far Away...' It is not just the styling of this film that looks backwards rather than forwards, so too do the underlining values and ideology. What I mean by this is that, in obvious ways, the supposedly far-future technology of *Star Wars* is actually old-fashioned, 1940s technology; for instance, the X-Wing fighters are WWII fighters and bombers. Scenes such as the one in which Luke and Obi-Wan go into the Mos Eisley bar are based on the ubiquitous bar-room scene of western movies. The reason for this, I think, is that it is precisely this bygone age of heroism that appeals to George Lucas, the director, and therefore to us, his audience. But this appeals to Lucas for a particular reason: that the political ideology underlying these films is profoundly conservative. This SF text is backward-looking in terms of its styling because its underlying value-structure is backward-looking. I shall say a little more about this later on.

However, it needs to be stressed that *Star Wars* laid the future foundations for SF in the 1980s and 1990s. Of course, the first reaction of the crowds queuing to see it in long lines outside cinemas in 1977 was not how old-fashioned it was, but how futuristic, how advanced and prophetic it looked. This is the way ideology masks itself: it pretends to be forward-looking to disguise its conservatism. But there is something more here: a sense in which this is the creative tension at the core of the *Star Wars* films, the contradiction that powers their unique appeal. The paradox is embodied by the new trilogy of films being made by Lucas, the first of which, *The Phantom Menace*, was released in 1999. Because the three new films are prequels, they are necessarily set back in the history of the *Star Wars* universe; and accordingly their styling and design must embody that history, must in some sense suggest 'old-fashionedness' when compared to the styling and design of the original movies. But because these films are actually being made twenty years *after* the original films – twenty years in which film technology, and especially the technology of special effects, have matured enormously – they are also, necessarily, going to look *more modern*, more up-to-date, more futuristic. Cinemagoers would be loath to pay to see a film that demonstrated 1950s-level special effects, although that would be one way of effectively retro-styling the movie. So the new *Star Wars* prequels embody a curious relation to history. They are simultaneously newer and older, more futuristic and more solidly set in the past. This curious circumstance neatly encapsulates the way any given SF text is positioned in relation to history and the future.

In a sense it is the contradictions of these films that give them so powerful and complex an appeal. There is, we can see, an unresolved tension between future-vision and past-vision that runs right through the original trilogy, and that manifests itself in, for instance, the way the films demonise technology. Technology is associated with the bad guys, the Empire: the Imperial stormtroopers are kitted up to look like robots; their all-machine worlds are entirely devoid of vegetation or any other organic, 'natural' landscaping; their enormous spaceships harness technology to immensely destructive ends. The rebels, on the other hand, are associated with forests and green colours, and most obviously with the organic 'Force' that supersedes the power of machines. But these are films that simultaneously relish and delight in their technology: the spectacle of their special effects, the delight of the spaceships and robots and all the *stuff*. As Scott

Bukatman puts it, the film evidences a 'struggle between antitechnological narrative and hyper-technological aesthetic' (Bukatman 1993: 347). What is interesting in this struggle is the way both the ubiquity of the technology and the universal immanence of the 'Force' enact a web of intertextual quotations and allusions that binds the whole text together. That is what these nova symbolise: the linkage and coherence of intertextuality itself, the web of quotation and allusion in which all texts are located.

It is hard to deny, certainly, that watching a film like *Star Wars* as an SF fan is a process of identifying a web of allusions and quotations from SF texts, particularly Golden Age texts. Lucas's first ambition was to make a modern version of the 1930s comic-strip and matinee film series *Flash Gordon*. He researched this idea, but abandoned it because the estate that owned the *Flash Gordon* copyright wanted too much money. Lacking that, Lucas invented his own imaginary universe, one that owes something to the mood and tone of *Flash Gordon* but which loses the elements of high camp fun that characterised the original. The feel of the *Star Wars* universe owes more to such Space Opera classic authors as Edgar Rice Burroughs and, especially, E E 'Doc' Smith, whose *Lensman* novels are evidently a direct source. Most obviously Smithian is the scale of Lucas's universe and the artefacts in it, in particular the 'Death Star', an entire artificial planet that destroys other planets. Smith wrote of an entire planet aimed and fired at Earth at faster-than-light speeds, like a vast cannonball. Lucas may also have been thinking of the AKKA, a super-weapon from Jack Williamson's *The Legion of Space* (1934), which exterminates whole fleets of spaceships at the push of a button.

Lucas also deliberately modelled his screenplay on a classic of Japanese cinema, Akira Kurosawa's *The Hidden Fortress* (1958), in which a Princess and her loyal General undertake a perilous quest to recover their rightful treasure, aided only by two bumbling and comical servants. Lucas has consistently expressed his admiration for Kurosawa as a film-maker, and in *Star Wars* he not only borrows specific elements of this film's narrative, most particularly the two servants who become the droids R2D2 and C3PO, but goes some way towards aping Kurosawa's characteristic epic-sweep directing style. Critics have spent some time on this high-culture source for *Star Wars*; but even this act of homage is part of a popular-culture Pulp-tradition: another Kurosawa film, *The Seven Samurai* (1954), was remade as the incomparable western *The Magnificent Seven* (1960). Of course, there is the element of the western in *Star Wars* too, and this helps give it its distinctively American tone. But surely more significant for the film is its heritage in films of the Second World War, most notably *The Dam Busters* (1954) and *633 Squadron* (1964), from which the film's ending is taken. It is WWII, and specifically its ethical contrast between the ideologies of the Allies and the Nazis, that gives *Star Wars* its moral framework. In particular, Peter Cushing's character Grand Moff Tarkin, with his Nazi-style uniform and his merciless style so evocative of war-film Nazi villains, helps link the Empire with that particular 1940s manifestation of evil.

Lucas also fills his film with explicit references to the traditions of American SF. The scenes shot on Tatooine, Luke Skywalker's homeworld, make very obvious reference to *Dune*: in fact, this (relatively brief) cinematic representation of a desert world is rather more powerful than David Lynch's feeble film of *Dune* (1984) itself. Also derived from Herbert's *Dune*, I think, is the blend of the East, in the guises of the patronising Bedouin variants, the Jawas, as well as the whole bag-and-baggage of 'the Force', which seems to me a translation into populist terms of Herbert's more arcane mysticism – and the West. Tatooine is the location for the frontiersmen and outlaws, like the wild west: Luke's father is a sodbuster, and the bar in Mos Eisley and Han Solo himself represent the gunslinger side of George Stevens's 1953 film *Shane*. Peter Nicholls thinks that Lucas's 'decadent

Galactic Empire' was 'perhaps inspired by Isaac Asimov's *Foundation* series' (Nicholls 1981: 571]. The Kurosawa-based robots certainly do owe a lot to Asimov, the formulator (with John Campbell) of the once-famous 'three laws of robotics' (see p. 158), which these robots seem to follow, and the writer of a great many novels and stories in which the 'humanity' of robots becomes a key feature. The alien 'Ewoks' in *Return of the Jedi*, little furry teddy-bear creatures who, with enormous implausibility, defeat the heavily armed and armoured shock troops of the Empire using clubs and stones in the trilogy's final battle – these Ewoks bear so close a resemblance to H Beam Piper's 'Fuzzies', from a series of novels that began with 1962's *Little Fuzzy*, that Piper's estate considered suing for breach of copyright.

SF intertextuality, then, is one of the key ways in which this film text operates, and our response to the film is conditioned by that fact. The intriguingly double-edged relationship of the film to its own imagined history, and to the history of the genre of which it is some sort of apotheosis, exemplifies the concerns of that history. To put this another way: one of the factors of SF fandom is an intimate knowledge of the canon and conventions of SF itself – in short, a knowledge of the history of the evolution of the form itself. This gives the initiate a double reading or viewing experience: the text, such as *Star Wars*, can be enjoyed on its own terms and simultaneously be enjoyed as a matrix of quotation, allusion, pastiche and reference. Many texts outside SF can be enjoyed in this latter manner, too, of course; but it is the intensity of the devotion of SF fans for their subject that permits these dense and sophisticated intertexts (texts that connect with many other texts) in a popular idiom. The SF text is both about its professed subject and also, always, *about SF*. This is where the points made in the first chapter come together. *Star Wars* is both forward-looking, which is to say futuristic, *and* backward-looking, or nostalgic, but SF's backward orientation means more than the fact that it is set 'a long time ago, in a galaxy far away'.

Star Wars looks backwards over the history of the genre itself, in that it incorporates Smith, Asimov, Herbert, *Flash Gordon* and more. It juxtaposes past and future so thoroughly, in so immanent a manner, that it inhabits the contradiction that is at the heart of any 'history of the future'. When this text makes reference to its all-powerful 'Force' that binds and connects everything, that controls the agents' actions but can also be controlled by them, that permits tremendous feats within the SF idiom, what it is really doing is invoking the imaginative potency of the genre within which it exists, the intertextual power of the science-fictional mode itself. This amounts to a definition of what the Force is: it is SF, linking and empowering the individual text across the network of SF history.

3

GENDER

One of the major theoretical projects of the second wave of feminism
is the investigation of gender and sexuality as social constructs...The
stock conventions of science fiction – time travel, alternate worlds,
entropy, relativism, the search for a unified field theory – can be used
metaphorically and metonymically as powerful ways of exploring the
construction of 'woman'.

(Sarah Lefanu 1988: 4–5)

FEMINIST SCIENCE FICTION

Women's science fiction, or feminist science fiction, is a more
recent development than the genre as a whole, but today constitutes one of the most exciting and most vigorous aspects of the
mode, in terms both of actual SF texts and of criticism. It is also,
following on from the previous chapter, a development that dates
primarily from the 1960s, one that has grown up in dialogue
with the more male-oriented SF of the Pulps and the Golden
Age. Examining some of the features of women's SF writing,
then, allows us to interrogate many aspects of New Wave (the
experimental, avant-garde movement in SF that started in the
1960s) and more recent developments in the mode.

After exploring various aspects of the representation of gender concerns in SF, this chapter will close with a reading of Ursula Le Guin's 1969 novel, *The Left Hand of Darkness*. But it is worth noting at the beginning how contentious Le Guin's position is within the body of female SF, as a means of pointing up that 'female SF' is not a straightforwardly or narrowly single quantity. *The Left Hand of Darkness* is one of the acknowledged classics of SF; it won, for instance, both a Hugo and a Nebula award, the two most prestigious awards in SF publishing. But much of the feminist criticism of Le Guin is rather cold, sometimes dismissive, and occasionally outright hostile. Critic Sarah Lefanu finds Le Guin's writing fatally limited, too character-based to be SF at all, and not very well realised as character studies either. Of the characters in *The Left Hand of Darkness* Lefanu asks 'how realistic are [they]? Who remembers what they look like? or what they say? Or feel?' (Lefanu 1988: 143). Lefanu prefers SF writer Joanna Russ. Joanna Russ herself thought *The Left Hand of Darkness* a failure, though an honourable one. Jenny Wolmark's *Aliens and Others: Science Fiction, Feminism and Postmodernism* (1994) omits Le Guin altogether, and the critic Susan Bassnett, whilst conceding that Le Guin has been 'extremely popular and successful' for 'both adults and children', none the less points out in Lucie Armitt's edited collection *Where No Man Has Gone Before* (1991) that she 'has not always been treated very kindly by those critics who have actually considered her work' (Armitt 1991: 50). There is a great deal of valuable criticism of SF from a feminist or women's writing point of view. In order to understand why as talented a writer as Le Guin has received such a poor showing in that criticism, and why her novels are so consistently judged in terms of her representation of gender, we need briefly to put her work into context.

One of the reasons why feminist criticism of SF has a radicalism that seems almost old-fashioned when compared with the subtler, more complex feminisms that characterise criticism as a whole is that women are a relatively recent arrival in the realm of SF writing itself. 'Golden Age' SF, the argument goes, was almost exclusively male; it was written by men, purchased by men or boys; its conventions were shaped by the passions and interests of adolescent males, that is to say its focus was on technology as embodied particularly by big, gleaming machines with lots of moving parts, physical prowess, war, two-dimensional male heroes, adventure and excitement. From the dawn of SF through to the end of the 1950s the female audience for SF was tiny, and those women who were interested in reading it did so with a sense of themselves as alienated or at least sidelined spectators. This is to skim swiftly over the surface of a large and complicated subject here, so a certain crudity of generalisation is inevitable; but it cannot be denied that the Golden Age readership of SF was predominantly, even overwhelmingly male; whereas the audience for SF today, particularly in America, is in the majority female. There are two things that account for this shift.

The first was the establishment, slowly at first but then, as it gained in popularity and sales, more rapidly, of a body of SF novels written by women and read in large part by women. This is something that happened particularly in the 1960s and 1970s, and there are three names associated with the success of this new mode. They are: Marion Zimmer Bradley, Andre Norton and Ursula Le Guin. Bradley has written dozens of novels set on a planet called Darkover, the chronicles of which span the world's history from a pre-technological, medievalised culture to a space-faring technological one. Andre Norton's series of Fantasy novels set on what she calls the *Witch World* provided the first, and one of the most popular, reworkings of the Tolkien style of Fantasy Epic from a female point of view. Ursula Le Guin has not written an on-going series of novels in the SF idiom, as have these other two, but her novels have included some of the most acclaimed works in SF, not only *The Left Hand of Darkness* but also *The Dispossessed* (1974) and her Fantasy sequence *Earthsea* (1968–90).

For our purposes the interesting thing about all three of these writers is the way they began by writing male-centred, techno-logical SF derived heavily from the Golden Age conventions, but as their confidence, and audience, grew, each of them shifted her perspective to female-centred studies that explored concerns more crucial to her own life. Marion Zimmer Bradley is one example of this. One of her earliest Darkover books, *Star of Danger* (1965), has a 'Boy's Own' plot about two young lads travelling through a wilderness area of the planet, undergoing a series of adventures whilst on the run from a bandit chief. There are no major female characters in this novel, and virtually no women of any sort. More than this, the protagonist, Larry Montry from Earth, falls under the spell of the unreconstructed machismo of Darkover culture. He meets a young nobleman of that world, Kennard Dalton, after bravely fighting off a gang of toughs. Triumphing in this fight wins Larry respect. Darkovans, or at any rate male Darkovans, find it incomprehensible that people on Earth rely on the police to sort out their difficulties: on Darkover, if an individual is wronged it is that individual's duty to obtain retribution. Earth's is 'a government of laws', but, says Kennard proudly, 'ours is a government of men, because laws can't be anything but the expression of men who make them' (Bradley 1965: 82). At no point in the novel are the masculinist prejudices of the Darkovian world challenged, or even mentioned without a sort of starry-eyed respect. But a later Darkover novel, *Stormqueen* (1978), is more women-oriented, and marks the feminist evolution of its author's sensibilities. It is set several hundred years before the Darkover of *Star of Danger*, in an age before the technologies of space flight have reached the planet, and it is far more explicit about the perils so macho a society involves for the women who live in it. One character, about to make a sort of marriage of con-venience to a powerful noble, explains to her son that 'life is not easy for a woman unprotected'. Without this unwanted marriage, the alternative would be an effective concubinage; 'for me there

would be nothing but to be a drudge or a sewing woman'
(Bradley 1978: 6). As the novel progresses, the main character
reveals telepathic capacities, known as *laran*, and the book
explores the compensations that *laran* offers to women in a brutal
and oppressive society. Bradley has talked about her shift of interests. In the introduction to *The Best of Marion Zimmer Bradley*, a
collection of her short fiction published in 1985, she said her
'current enthusiasms…are Gay Rights and Women's Rights – I
think Women's Liberation is the great event of the twentieth century, not Space Exploration. One is a great change in human consciousness; the latter is only predictable technology, and I am
bored by technology' (Bradley 1985: 13).

This emphasis on the affective, the personal, rather than the
technological was also the reason for the second significant catalyst from the 1960s, one that introduced a large body of female
fans to SF, fans that had previously been put off by the masculinist 'boys and their toys' posturings of Golden Age books. This
catalyst was the TV series *Star Trek*. Indeed, although its importance is often underplayed, it seems clear to me that *Star Trek*
brought more women to SF than all the other authors mentioned
so far put together. It remains a cornerstone of female SF fandom.
The success of this syndicated show in the late sixties, particularly amongst a female audience, brought hundreds of thousands
of women to the genre. And this was a success based less on the
technological or male-ego strands of the show, and had more to
do with the way *Star Trek* represented, in the first instance,
human interaction and the social dynamic as being at the heart of
the SF story; and, in the second instance, and less obviously,
because *Trek*, unusually for a 1960s US TV show, was interested
in representing difference. The encounter with the alien is at the
core of *Star Trek*, and of most SF; and questions of difference, of
alien-ness and otherness, were also powerful and relevant to the
female perspective on the old patriarchal world. This is why the
show built up, and maintains, so large a female audience. Nor is

this female audience merely a body of passive viewers; there is a vigorous and wide-ranging body of fanzines and even fan-authored novels based upon the *Star Trek* universe. As Henry Jenkins has exhaustively demonstrated, '*Star Trek* fandom is a predominantly female response to mass media texts, with the majority of fanzines edited by and written by women for a largely female readership' (Tulloch and Jenkins 1995: 196–7).

It was this issue of difference, where 'alien' becomes an encoding of 'woman', that featured prominently in the work of the 1970s new wave of radical female SF writers. This was a much more populated era of women's SF in terms of the number of women writing SF. But there are three names that crop up again and again in the criticism, so I mention them here: Octavia Butler, Marge Piercy and Joanna Russ. Russ is perhaps the most often cited. Her most famous novel, *The Female Man* (1975), presents a four-fold perspective of women's experience of the world, including a women-only utopian realm called Whileaway. Russ is one of the most committed feminist writers and critics, and *The Female Man* has received a great deal of respectful criticism. But Gwyneth Jones is surely right when she judges this novel a relative failure compared with some others of Russ's fictions. It is set partly on the planet Whileaway where there are no men, only women, and the utopian possibilities of this world are contrasted with the trajectories of female existence on other possible worlds where women are oppressed to one degree or another. Russ has written about all-female societies elsewhere, most notably in the story 'When It Changed' (1972), but, as Jones points out, the female society in that story is 'not unreasonably idealised'. The women have the faults and strengths of 'the whole of humanity'. By the time of *The Female Man* the all-woman world 'has been got at. Its inhabitants have become female characters in a feminist science fiction, their vices and virtues bowdlerised and engineered precisely to fit the current demands of sexual politics.' Russ's novel is effectively hijacked by a feminist agenda: '*When It*

Changed is feminist fiction, *The Female Man* is feminist satire' (Jones 1999: 125–6).

Of the other names mentioned, Octavia Butler, as a writer both female and black, has an especially acute perspective on issues of 'alien as other'. Her *Xenogenesis* series is examined in Chapter 4 of the present study. Marge Piercy's feminist utopia *Woman on the Edge of Time* (1976) is often contrasted with *The Left Hand of Darkness* as a 'successful' version of a world without gender. Another name worth introducing at this point, although not one that seems immediately appropriate in a discussion of SF written by women, is James Tiptree Jr. Despite having the first name James, Tiptree has the distinction of having created one of the most celebrated fictional expressions of the constructions of gender, in a short story called 'The Women Men Don't See' (1973). This tale is narrated by a man called Fenton, rather old-fashioned but basically decent, whose blindness to the actual conditions of what it means to be a woman, as opposed to his vague sense of what he *thinks* women are about, is the key point of the story. Indeed, the triumph of Tiptree's narration is the way it captures so precisely the idiom of a certain sort of male consciousness, whilst also using *only* that blinkered male point of view to delineate the women as separate characters. The story opens on a small aeroplane flying down to Mexico.

> I see her first while the Mexicana 727 is barrelling down to Cozumel Island. I come out of the can and lurch into her seat, saying 'Sorry,' at a double female blur. The second blur nods quietly. The younger one in the window seat goes on looking out. I continue down the aisle registering nothing. Zero. I would never have looked at them or thought of them again.
>
> (Tiptree, *Warm Worlds and Otherwise* (1979): 131)

The plane crashes, and the narrator and the two women are forced to fend for themselves. But the story takes a striking turn when space aliens encounter them in the jungle. 'They are tall and white...stretching out a long white arm toward Ruth...the arm stretches after her. It stretches and stretches. It stretches two yards and stays hanging in the air. Small black things are wriggling from its tip. I look where their faces should be and see black hollow dishes with vertical stripes' (p. 156). The narrator's response is a male one: full of terror he fires his gun at the aliens. The women are more pragmatic. They announce they are going to leave the planet with them. 'For Christ's sake, Ruth, they're *aliens*,' yells Fenton. 'I'm used to it,' Ruth replies. Ruth's point of view is that the aliens are just as men were on Earth, and that women are used to the marginal existence: 'we survive by ones or twos in the chinks of your world machine' (pp. 160–4). The aliens themselves, with their weird technology and their satellite-dish faces, seem to embody a particular, technological metaphor for maleness; just as their spaceship, a piece of technology, is no more of a 'world machine' than the machinery of patriarchy. Women's marginal role in this machine-system manages to reverse the woman-as-alien motif. From the perspective of Ruth, a space alien is not more alien than a man.

This is a story, though, celebrated for more than literary reasons. To quote Edward James:

> Robert Silverberg commented that this ['The Women Men Don't See'] was 'a profoundly feminist story told in an entirely masculine manner,' and a few pages earlier in his introduction to the collection which included this story he remarked: 'It has been suggested that Tiptree is female, a theory I find absurd, for there is to me something ineluctably masculine about Tiptree's writing.' It was not just the writing, but the lifestyle. Silverberg noted how Tiptree in a letter had admitted to having worked in a Pentagon basement during the war and to having subsequently 'batted around the jungly parts of the globe.'
>
> (James 1994: 186)

As James points out, this whole affair is especially involving to 'those interested in the difference between "masculine" and "feminine" writing (like Le Guin and Silverberg himself)', because, of course, James Tiptree Jr was a woman called Alice Sheldon, a fact which finally emerged in 1977. The embarrassment of the more chauvinist SF writers, such as Silverberg or Heinlein, at this admission was met by the delight of the more feminist critics and authors; it seemed to crystallise the ingrained sexism of assumptions governing different sorts of writing, as well as emphasising how alive this issue was. In the fiery heat of 1970s-style feminism, this was a crucial issue.

The Tiptree situation in some senses harked back to an earlier age. I have talked of the 1960s as the time when female SF really increased in popularity, yet, as Sarah Lefanu has noted, the situation was not quite as clearcut as that:

> Science fiction is popularly conceived as male territory, boys' own adventure stories with little to interest a female readership. This is true of the heyday of magazine science fiction, the 1930s and 1940s, but even then there were women writers, like C L Moore and Leigh Brackett.
>
> (Lefanu 1988: 2)

The difference, she points out, is that such women more often than not 'assumed a male voice and non-gender-specific names to avoid prejudice on the part of editors and readers alike'. Women who wished to become involved, as writers or readers, had to assume a certain masculine identity, to become what we might call (after Russ's novel), Female Men. The Tiptree experiment in a sense focused exactly these prejudices, but at a more gender-aware time.

What Tiptree does, as Le Guin, Butler and Russ have also done in their various ways, is precisely to use the SF encounter with difference to focus gender concerns. An essay by Russ that was first published in the SF magazine *Vertex* in 1971 is often cited by feminist critics of SF as a classic articulation of these issues. In that essay, Russ declared that 'one would think science fiction the perfect literary mode in which to explore (and explode) our assumptions about "innate" values and "natural" social arrangements'. But whilst 'some of this has been done', Russ points out that 'speculation about the innate personality differences between men and women, about family structure, about sex, in short about gender roles, does not exist at all'. The essay is called 'The Image of Women in Science Fiction'; Russ says she chose that title rather than 'Women in Science Fiction' because 'if I had chosen the latter, there would have been very little to say. There are plenty of images of women in science fiction. There are hardly any women' (Russ 1972: 79–80). It can be argued that now, thirty years later, the situation is not quite so bleak as it was then. But there is still a sense in which the SF contact with the alien remains a powerful medium for expressing female perspectives.

WOMEN AND ALIENS

The point here, as throughout this study, is not that SF articulates the difference of women in the sense that women 'are different' from men. There is SF that basically says just that, but it is not SF properly located in the discourse of difference; instead it is simply a means of reinstating the 'normality' of the male experience, and the 'deviance from the norm' that is women, and it therefore remains a sexist discourse. A genuine discourse of alterity would examine the ways gender constructs difference, the way a person's gender is conceived in terms of difference. It might use an expression of material difference, which is to say, non-humanity – a space alien, a machine, a symbolic novum – as a means of exploring what it is like to have the label 'different' imposed on a person by some normalising system.

These are some of the ways 'the alien' can be used to encode the female experience. Marleen Barr has talked about the way 'the female' in patriarchal society is already constituted as alien: women are 'alien in our culture which insists that "to be human is to be male"' (Barr 1987: 31). Robin Roberts, in her book *A New Species* (1993), has looked in detail at the way 'the alien' has been used to figure female experience. Jenny Wolmark has also worked through this theme, bringing in some of the insights of postmodern theory. Wolmark finds merit in those books that challenge the more reactionary SF notion of 'alien' as villain, the sort of representation to be found in texts such as Robert Heinlein's *Starship Troopers* (1959), in which a quasi-fascist military society is engaged in a prolonged and bloody interstellar war against repulsive giant insectoid aliens. Heinlein's giant bugs are one apotheosis of 'the enemy': they have none of the qualities humanity has traditionally valued, qualities like compassion, intellect, culture, spirituality, and they are unambiguously devoted to the violent destruction of our kind. They are also hive creatures, without a separate, individual existence. For readers who share Heinlein's right-wing libertarian politics, especially those readers of the 1950s or 1960s, they are easily read as a straightforward code for 'communists'. For many women, SF that writes this sort of opposition is too facile. In a discussion of the novels of Gwyneth Jones and Octavia Butler, Wolmark observes:

> The science fiction convention of the alien attempts to present otherness in unitary terms, so that 'humanity' is uncomplicatedly opposed to the 'alien'; both Jones and Butler focus on the way in which the opposition seeks to suppress the others of both gender and race by subsuming them within a common-sense notion of what it is to be human.
>
> (Wolmark 1994: 46)

This complexity goes deeper than might at first be thought. Very little SF, even in the depths of male-authored Pulps, advances a 'common-sense notion of what it is to be human'; and consequently representations of the 'alien' are very rarely as straightfor-wardly demonised as Heinlein's repulsive insect foe from *Starship Troopers*. Most aliens embody some degree of awareness of difference, which might be encoded in various ways such as race, culture or gender.

An example of the encoding of gender might be found in the *Alien* films. This is a series that has become increasingly identified with one of its female characters, Ripley, as played by Sigourney Weaver. Ripley is a 'strong' woman in all four films, self-reliant and motivated to survive. Each of the four films shares the same basic premise: the encounter with a monstrous Other, an alien who kills and mutilates. The gender identity of this beast seems straightforward enough: in the first film, *Alien*, it is an aggressive male, attacking and killing, penetrating its victims in a violent coding of rape with a monstrous toothed phallus that protrudes from its mouth. This same 'male' also impregnates some of its victims, placing a baby alien in their bellies, be they male or female: a symbolic death-fetus that is born by fatally bursting through the torso. But as the series progresses, this gender identification becomes problematised, partly through an identification with Ripley herself, such that the alien becomes a more extreme version of the woman. Ripley is tall and strong, but the alien is taller and stronger; Ripley survives in a series of ingenious ways, the alien survives more extreme threats. For instance in *Aliens*, the second film, it survives even hanging outside a spacecraft in space. In *Aliens*, Ripley is maternal, protecting 'Newt', a little girl who is the sole survivor of the alien attack; but the Queen alien whom Ripley confronts is even more maternal, with a nest of 'thousands' of children, or eggs, which Ripley must try to destroy. Indeed, some critics argue that the alien, despite its various 'masculine' attributes, is representative throughout the films of 'the monstrous feminine'. Barbara Creed, for instance, points out that in *Alien* 'virtually all aspects of the *mise-en-scene* are designed to signify the female: womb-like interiors, fallopian tube corridors, small claustrophobic spaces', going on to argue that in contemporary culture 'the body, particularly the woman's body, has come to signify the unknown, the terrifying, the monstrous' (in Kuhn 1990: 215–16). By the third film, the identification of alien with woman, and of Ripley with alien, is becoming more explicit. 'The Bitch Is Back' announced the poster publicity for this film, over a double shot of Ripley and the alien confronting one another, the slogan apparently referring to either, or both, of them. By *Alien 4*, Ripley and the alien have literally become one; reconstructed from contaminated DNA, Ripley becomes a woman–alien hybrid. In all of these films, there is an acute turning-away from men; all the men die in the first film, although Ripley is able to save the cat; all but one die in the second (and he dies shortly after), although Ripley does save the small girl; in the third film, men are represented exclusively by criminals, rapists and outcasts, all but one of whom are killed; by the fourth movie the Ripley–alien struggles to save the life of the only other survivor from two separate spacecraft: a female android. There is a balance of horror and delight in the man-killing actions of the alien, both visceral distaste for the bloodshed and a certain admiration for the beauty and form of the alien itself, its instinctual ingenuity, its grace. It is a sort of aggressive compensatory fantasy, a woman who rapes but cannot be raped: if penetrated, the alien spurts disfiguring acid, something that wounds many characters in the films – all of whom are men.

From the point of view of gender representation, the effect of these four extremely popular films taken together is the strength given to positive representations of the female by so monstrous an embodiment of alterity as the alien monster it(her)self. The identification of the monster with 'femaleness' inverts some of the traditional sexist assumptions about what women are like. It is strong, violent, active rather than passive, and the fetishisation of that very monster, evidenced for instance by fannish obsession with the H R Geiger designs that shaped it, celebrates the bursting of traditional bounds. The *Alien* films eventually reveal themselves as being about hybridisation, with the Ripley/alien dual-creature the only surviving organism, about to reach Earth and presumably spread her radically different DNA over the planet.

This celebration of the hybrid is one of the main strands of strong female SF, and in part it provides a direct access to the poetics of alterity. Sheri Tepper's novel *Grass* (1989) sets itself up as a sort of futuristic fairytale. Conventional wife and mother Marjorie Westriding goes with her husband and children to the planet Grass in search of a cure for a devastating galactic plague. There she encounters an aristocratic culture dedicated to hunting foxes; except that the 'foxen' they hunt are actually enormous alien monsters who provide no clear outline to the eye but give a terrifying impression of claws and teeth. The 'horses' ridden by the human settlers are alien too, the Hippae, muscular and sharp-toothed. As the novel progresses, it becomes apparent that it is the Hippae who are ruling the occasion, telepathically compelling the human riders to help them hunt down and kill their enemies, the foxen. The human interest of the narrative traces out a story where, like a good feminist heroine, Westriding rebels against the strictness of her religious upbringing and turns against her husband's infidelity. But it is the end of the novel that is most striking, and the place where the encounter with difference is most dramatically realised: Marjorie Westriding does not choose to fall in love with the handsome human alternatives to her husband, nor to live independently (a common motif in feminist fiction), but instead falls in love with one of the foxen, and rides away on him through an inter-dimensional portal. It is 'Beauty and the Beast', except that the beast not only remains a beast at the end of the tale, it is his very bestiality, his irreducible otherness, that is the reason she falls in love with him. As

Marleen Barr puts it, 'Marjorie learns that her ultimate emotional experience involves loving foxen while she is located outside patriarchy, not hunting them to prove her manhood. She chooses to love a male Other to manhood whose species is persecuted in the name of proving manhood. She experiences splendour in the grass with an alien' (Barr 1987: 132).

Critic and theorist Donna Harraway has written an influential essay that celebrates exactly the feminist potential of this sort of hybridisation, focused for her by the figure of the Cyborg. Part organic, part machine, the cyborg has been a common theme in SF for many decades. More often than not, SF cyborgs are menacing, like the Daleks of *Dr Who* or the Borg of *Star Trek*. By reclaiming the trope of the cyborg as a feminist icon, Harraway is perfectly aware that she is being controversial, or, as she puts it, 'ironic' and 'blasphemous'. But her celebration of the feminist possibilities of the hybridisation of the cyborg has struck a chord with many thinkers, and not only feminist ones. Her point is initially that, as human beings who rely on machinery to an intimate and unprecedented degree, we (she is addressing herself to women) are already cyborgs; that 'the boundary between science fiction and social reality is an optical illusion' because 'the cyborg is a matter of fiction and lived experience that changes what counts as women's experience in the late twentieth-century' (Harraway 1991: 149). Her examples begin with real life, the commonplace cyborgs created by medicine, production, war and everyday life. The 'I' that is addressing you now, for instance, is only able to do so as a cyborg amalgamation of my flesh and the various machinery of computing, book-production and distribution. Harraway then moves seamlessly on to the representation of cyborgs in science fiction, in which a variety of (mostly) female authors is lauded for creating 'a myth about identity and boundaries which might inform late twentieth-century political imaginations' (Harraway 1991: 173). It is the range of her examples as much as anything that is so significant: from the high feminist art of Joanna Russ's *The Female Man* to the complex highbrow Science Fantasy of Samuel Delany's *Nevèrÿon* sequence, to the right-wing Hard SF of John Varley, and the populist writing of Anne McCaffrey. The books in Varley's trilogy, *Titan*, *Wizard* and *Demon*, are all set aboard an enormous part-organic part-technological space station/world in the shape of an enormous wheel orbiting Jupiter. McCaffrey's *The Ship Who Sang* (1969) is about a handicapped girl whose mind is transferred into a spaceship. It is the diversity of this list of examples that is its point as much as anything. The cyborg may be monstrous, in the same way that the *Alien* is monstrous, or magnificent; but the crucial thing about it is that it is the site of the encounter with difference. In the words of Jane Donawerth, 'stories of alien women in science fiction by women thus take on, unmetaphor, and live out the cultural stereotypes of women. In each case, the narratives confront and transform the stereotypes' (Donawerth 1997: 107–8). This process of 'unmetaphoring', of unpacking and making explicit the metaphors by which stereotypes work, is exactly the strength of SF as a materialist mode of writing. Instead of presenting woman as a metaphorical alien in contemporary society, an SF text can present an *actual* woman (like Ripley) as an *actual* alien; can attack the stereotype in a more direct, more vivid and more powerful manner.

CASE STUDY: URSULA LE GUIN, *THE LEFT HAND OF DARKNESS* (1969)

Few works of SF, or of any literature, explore questions of gender as profoundly as Le Guin's masterpiece *The Left Hand of Darkness* (1969). The plot of Le Guin's novel is easily summarised, and is according to some the least interesting aspect of the work. Genly Ai is an ambassador from the Hainish Ekumensis, who has come by himself to the world of Gethen, also known as Winter, with the aim of introducing that world to the spacefaring cultures of his interstellar commonwealth. Such ambassadors come alone, in order not to intimidate the home culture. Genly Ai comes first of all to the nation of Karhide, where he is befriended by the prime minister Estraven; but Karhide's king is mad, and more than a little paranoid. He banishes Estraven for treason, and rejects Genly Ai's mission. Genly then leaves Karhide and travels to the neighbouring nation of Orgoreyn, moving from a 'Western'-style culture to an Iron Curtain-vintage Eastern European one, a state bureaucracy, the second of the two superpowers of Gethen. Estraven has also fled here, and he and Genly Ai meet up again. Although the Orgoreyns seem initially favourable to Genly's mission, their thoughts are actually on an impending war with their neighbouring country. Genly and Estraven are thrown into a Siberian-style prison; they escape, and embark on a huge trek across the winter ice-deserts, slowly and heroically making their way through appalling conditions back to Karhide on the other side of the world. At the end of this trek Estraven is killed, but Genly Ai makes it back to find the king now favourably disposed to his mission. The novel ends with Gethen, Winter, accepting further representations from the Ekumensis.

Critical attention on this novel has concentrated less on this storyline, and more on the novel's premise. But in fact it is more correct to talk of the novel's two premises. The first is the climactic premise; Le Guin has imagined a world perennially stuck in winter. This is a winter planet, in the way that Herbert's *Dune* is a desert planet; indeed, Le Guin's conception probably owes much to Herbert's vision of climate shaping culture. On this planet it is cold during summer, and the winters plunge the world into astonishing snowstorms and lows of temperature. It is difficult to avoid the sense that everything that happens on Gethen is primarily shaped by the weather. Society has evolved out of close-knit communities called Hearths, partly familial partly tribal, where people gather together against the cold. Everything from the architecture to the religion reflects the constraints of the weather. As Genly says himself, 'Winter is an inimical world; its punishment for doing wrong is sure and prompt.' Expulsion from the Hearths leads to 'death from cold, death from hunger' (Le Guin, *The Left Hand of Darkness* (1969): 88). The resulting society is close knit, and regulated by complex social codes of 'face' or 'honour': *shifgrethor* as it is called.

But it is the second premise of the novel that has attracted the most critical attention, and that has the most obvious feminist implications. The world of Gethen, or Winter, has no fixed gender; nobody on this planet is 'male' or 'female'. Instead, all Gethenians live according to a monthly cycle. For most of this cycle, they are neither male nor female, but sexless, or genderless, human beings. The technical term for this is androgyny, although the word implies being both sexually male and female, and this is not strictly the situation. For most of their lives, Gethenians are neither male nor female. Once a month or so they enter a period called *kemmer*.

> In the first phase of kemmer, the individual remains completely androgynous. Gender, and potency, are not achieved in isolation...Yet the sexual impulse is tremendously strong in this phase, controlling the entire personality...When the individual finds a partner in kemmer, hormonal secretion is further stimulated...until in one partner either a male or female hormonal dominance is established. The genitals engorge or shrink accordingly, foreplay intensifies, and the partner, triggered by the change, takes on the other sexual role...Normal individuals have no predisposition to either sexual role in kemmer; they do not know whether they will be the male or the female, and have no choice in the matter...[kemmer] ends fairly abruptly, and if conception has not taken place, the individual returns to the latent phase and the cycle begins anew. If the individual was in the female role and was impregnated, hormonal activity of course continues, and for the gestation

period the individual remains female...With the cessation of lactation the female becomes once more a perfect androgyne. No physiological habit is established, and the mother of several children may be the father of several more.

(Le Guin, *The Left Hand of Darkness* (1969): 82–3)

In her 1976 essay 'Is Gender Necessary?', a meditation upon her novel, Le Guin ponders 'why did I invent these peculiar people? Not just so that the book could contain, halfway through it, the sentence: "the king was pregnant" – although I admit I am fond of that sentence' (Le Guin 1989: 137). The sentence seems to capture the point of the experiment; it contradicts our assumptions. Kings do not get pregnant, partly because they are male and men do not have the physiological capacity for pregnancy, but also because a 'king' is an icon of masculine power, and it somehow diminishes our conception of that power to imagine it subject to the physical change of pregnancy.

In other words, in *The Left Hand of Darkness* Le Guin has hit upon a means of exploring the ways that gender, and our assumptions about gender, shapes the world we live in. In a sense this is the fundamental feminist project: not a raising up of women at the expense of men, but a trying to see beyond the mystifications of gender-related ideology. Try the thought experiment: how greatly does the sex of the person you are talking to, or living with, or watching on television, determine the ways you respond? How might a world without gender work? Chapter 7 of Le Guin's novel is called 'The Question of Sex', and pinpoints some of the answers to these sorts of question.

Anyone can turn his hand to anything. This sounds very simple, but its psychological effects are incalculable. The fact that everyone between seventeen and thirty-five or so is liable to be...'tied down to childbearing', implies that no one is quite so thoroughly 'tied down' here as women, elsewhere, are likely to be – psychologically and physically.

...A child has no pyscho-sexual relationship to his mother and father. There is no myth of Oedipus on Winter.

...There is no division of humanity into strong and weak halves, protected/protective, dominant/submissive, owner/chattel, active/passive. In fact the whole tendency to dualism that pervades human thinking may be found to be lessened, or changed, on Winter.

(Le Guin, *The Left Hand of Darkness* (1969): 84–5)

This last point is particularly interesting aesthetically. It is true that *Left Hand of Darkness* is remarkably non-binary as a novel. This may be one reason why some critics like it so little. It is not an exaggeration to suggest that most of our literary tradition, certainly in the novel, has come out of a binary aesthetic. Texts are very frequently structured around binary oppositions such as 'good versus evil', as for example in Milton's *Paradise Lost* or the novels of Dickens. Indeed some critics (for instance, Harold Bloom, in his book *Agon*) have argued that such binarism, or more specifically the conflict inherent in such opposition, is the root of the energy and appeal of literature. According to this model, Le Guin's text is something out of the ordinary. The novel contains little narrative tension, for instance. The larger question of whether Winter will join the Ekumensis is short-circuited early on in the book, when Genly Ai consults a Gethenian oracle and asks, precisely, that question. He is answered 'yes', and so it transpires. Predicting the future is not a matter of guesswork on Winter, but is rather a certainty. This does not, however, function in Gethenian culture as a Pandoran curse. The oracles are calm, as are most people on this world. Genly Ai tries to put across to one of these future-tellers how startling this is to him.

'Faxe, tell me this. You Handdarata have a gift that men on every world have craved. You have it. You can predict the

future. And yet you live like the rest of us – it doesn't seem to
matter –'

'Why should it matter, Genry?'

(Le Guin, The Left Hand of Darkness (1969): 64)

Genly is always coming across the Karhide verbal shrug-of-the-
shoulders, 'nusuth', a word which means 'what does it matter' or
'it doesn't matter'. It is as if, without the tension of fixed gender,
the inhabitants of this world have achieved a greater degree of
Zen-like acceptance about the cosmos. Although *The Left Hand of
Darkness* is essentially the tale of two characters – Genly Ai, from
offworld, and the native Estraven – and although we might
assume they are very different beings from entirely different
backgrounds, in fact Genly and Estraven seem very similar. The
book tells the story of their bonding, their closeness, and the sor-
row of Genly at Estraven's death. Their cultures may be different,
but their individuality doesn't seem to be. On a larger level, the
work is structured about two cultures, the 'Western' Karhide and
the 'Eastern' Orgoreyn; and here the differences are apparently
fairly pronounced. But because Winter society is rooted not in
any notion of nationhood, something which is consistently shown
to be a recent development in this ancient culture, and more on
the Hearth, on the individual relations between people, there is
precious little tension here either. Le Guin herself has said that
one of the initial impulses to write this novel came out of a desire
to write a world that knew nothing of war.

> At the very inception of the whole book, I was interested in
> writing a novel about people in a society that had never had a
> war. That came first. The androgyny came second. (Cause and
> effect? Effect and cause?)

(Le Guin 1989: 141)

Le Guin suggests that the warlessness of Winter is possibly the ultimate function of a genderless society, and by implication that war is nothing but a result of the fixed-gender nature of our own world. An interesting notion, this, but, it might be argued, perhaps aesthetically deadening. War, as the apotheosis, has been the engine of literature at least since the *Iliad*. But this is precisely what makes *The Left Hand of Darkness* such an expert performance: it achieves its gripping, finely detailed vision of alterity without resorting to over-obvious tactics of narrative or character opposition.

On the other hand, Le Guin's 'genderless' conception of the world has come in for some fierce criticism, particularly from feminist writers. The brunt of this criticism has to do with her project of the elimination of gender – that it is not that there is no gender on Winter, it is that there are no *women* on Winter. In part this has to do with the vexed question of the non-specific pronoun. Characters throughout the novel are called 'he'; the 'he/him/his' bias of the narrative is something Le Guin herself has subsequently regretted. She acknowledges that 'the Gethenians seem like men, instead of menwomen.' In her 1976 essay on the book, she explained, 'I call the Gethenians "he" because I utterly refuse to mangle English by inventing a pronoun for "he/she".' Her 1987 revision of this essay backtracks: 'This "utter refusal" of 1968 restated in 1976 collapsed, utterly, within a couple of years more. I still dislike invented pronouns, but now dislike them less than the so-called generic pronoun "he/him/his", which does in fact exclude women from discourse; and which was an invention of male grammarians in the sixteenth century' (Le Guin 1989: 145).

Perhaps Le Guin is being unnecessarily hard on herself. If the Gethenians are portrayed largely as male, this has surely to do with the perspective of the male Genly Ai, which in turn says less about Winter and more about genderist assumptions from outside the world. Genly is narrator: it is Genly who chooses to call the monarch 'king'. The novel begins with an elaborately described procession, full of pomp and the rituals of power, and all is described in terms of the 'male' gender: king, men, lords, mayors and so on. At one point, Estraven invites Genly to supper as part of the complex power games of the city. Genly tells us he was 'annoyed by this sense of effeminate intrigue' (*Left Hand*, p. 14). Within a few pages, the narrator (not the author) has set up a pattern of good/bad, male/female binarisms. But one of the subtleties of the novel is to unravel the common preconceptions that power is somehow masculine and that relationships are somehow feminine. Estraven seems unambiguously a man: 'one of the most powerful men in the country...He is lord of a Domain and lord of the Kingdom, a mover of great events' (p. 12), The king, in the impressive march of Chapter 1, is described in masculine terms. But by Chapter 3, when the king's paranoia becomes clearer, Genly's audience with him sees a shifting of gender. 'Agraven was less kingly, less manly, than he looked at a distance among his courtiers...He laughed shrilly like an angry woman pretending to be amused' (p. 33). In this case, the negative associations of the adjectives connect with a common discourse that sees madness, or hysteria, as something more female than male. But the striking first sentence of Chapter 5, 'My landlady, a voluble man...' helps isolate the fact that the sexism here is Genly's, not the author's. The 'landlady' is a father not a mother, but Genly jumps to gender conclusions even when they flatly contradict the physical facts. 'He was so feminine in looks and manner that I once asked him how many children he had. He looked glum. He had never borne any. He had, however, sired four' (p. 47). By the time we have followed the narrative through to Genly and Estraven's heroic trek across the ice, questions of gender have largely been bleached from the novel. Estraven actually goes into kemmer during this journey, and since Genly is permanently male (a 'pervert' in Gethenian terms) this means Estraven is a 'she'. Certainly by its closing pages *The Left Hand of Darkness* has become a sort of inter-racial love story; but one of the beauties of this is that we are left uncertain about whether to read the unconsummated love between Genly and Estraven as homosexual or heterosexual.

In 'Is Gender Necessary?', Le Guin admits that 'one does not see Estraven as a mother, with his children, in any role that we automatically perceive as "female": and therefore, we tend to see him as a man. This is a real flaw in the book, and I can only be very grateful to those readers, men and women, whose willingness to participate in the experiment led them to fill in that omission with the work of their own imagination' (Le Guin 1989: 146). This is crucial, I think; and one of the reasons *The Left Hand of Darkness* works so well is precisely that the creation of this imaginary world is so detailed and so compelling that readers are prompted to enter into the experiment fully. But in 1987 this position no longer satisfied Le Guin. She argued:

> I now see it thus: Men were inclined to be satisfied with the book, which allowed them a safe trip into androgyny and back from a conventionally male viewpoint. But many women wanted it to go further, to dare more, to explore androgyny from a woman's point of view as well as a man's...I think women were justified in asking more courage of me and a more rigorous thinking-through of implications.
>
> (Le Guin, 1989: 146)

But it might be better to represent the splitting of gender as working in a slightly different way. Joanna Russ sees Winter as being a community of men without women; we might with equal justification see it as a community of women without men. After all, the Gethenians are subject to a monthly cycle, as women are; all are liable to become pregnant and none of them have external genitalia: Estraven notes of the male Genly, 'there is a frailty about him. He is all unprotected, exposed, vulnerable, even to his sexual organ which he must carry always outside himself' (*Left Hand*, p. 194). When Genly tries to comprehend their society, he mostly reaches for female metaphors. The Hearth is a local group, like a family, which is supportive, nurturing. 'On Gethen,' Genly observes, 'nothing led to war. Quarrels, murders, feuds, forays...They lacked, it seemed, the capacity to mobilize. They behaved like animals in this respect, or women. They did not behave like men, or ants' (p. 47). The masculine element in the equation is the weather; comprised of vicious, sometimes hellish winter storms and wastelands through which Estraven and Genly battle in the latter sections of the novel.

The question that needs addressing, perhaps, is whether *The Left Hand of Darkness*'s twin premises can be aesthetically connected. Why does it follow that a book about a society without gender must also be a book about a society that lives in a perpetual winter? Several answers suggest themselves. Gwyneth Jones thinks that the icescapes of the novel reflect the intrusion into the centre of the narrative of the only man, Genly Ai: as if the novel is saying 'to become a woman is to *lose face*, to lose persona; to give up the role of the protagonist. This loss...is the blank ice' of the novel's world (Jones 1999: 205). Alternatively, perhaps Le Guin instinctively sought a landscape of ice and waste to dramatise a society without change, without flux. The necessary corollary of the Gethenian warlessness is a resistance to change; this is a society that has reached levels of technology equivalent to that of our 1960s, but has failed to advance beyond it: 'the mechanical–industrial Age of Invention in Karhide is at least three thousand years old' (*Left Hand*, p. 31). There is no war, and accordingly there is no progress. In 'Is Gender Necessary?', Le Guin even talks of this as one of the positive aspects of the society:

> The Gethenians [lacking 'masculinity'] do not rape their world. They have developed a high technology, heavy industry, automobiles, radios, explosives, etc., but they have done so very slowly, absorbing their technology rather than letting it

overwhelm them. They have no myth of progress at all.

(Le Guin 1989: 141)

Le Guin casts this as a function of gender, but it might be possible to see it as being part of a broader science-fictional suspicion of technology, the nostalgic, backward-looking machine phobia that has informed almost all the books we have looked at. But Le Guin's artistry is more than her ideology. There is something appealing about the world of Gethen, but there is something stagnant there too. As we learn right at the beginning, the Gethenians have no linear calendar, but reckon each year as Year One. 'It is always Year One here. Only the dating of every past and future year changes each New Year's day, as one counts backwards or forwards from the unitary Now' (*Left Hand*, p. 9).

That Le Guin manages to make this frozen society, this genderless social wasteland, so powerfully engaging is the great triumph of her art. And I think it has to do with the way she harks back to a far older culture than most SF. Although Gethen is backward-looking for an SF novel in terms of the technology it uses, it is even more nostalgic, even more retrograde, in its overall themes. The interspersed tales from Gethenian folklore are examples of the most primitive form of discourse there is, oral tales. Estraven tells an audience...

The whole tale of our crossing the ice. He told it as only a person of an oral-literature tradition can tell a story, so it became a saga, full of traditional locations and even episodes, yet exact and vivid, from the sulphurous fire and dark of the pass between Drumner and Dremegole to the screaming gusts from mountain-gaps that swept the bay of Guthen.

(Le Guin, *The Left Hand of Darkness* (1969): 232)

Le Guin is talking about her own technique here. She conveys her story not as if she is inventing a new narrative, but as if she is relating an ancient tale. The backward-looking rootedness of American SF in a primitive myth-aesthetic is very evident in this work.

Hand in hand with this is Le Guin's spirituality. Like 'the Force' in the equally mythic-aesthetic *Star Wars*, or the Bene Gesserit Sisterhood in Herbert's *Dune*, there is a strand of mysticism running throughout the otherwise rationalist fabric of the text. As has been mentioned, the Getherians are able to tell the future; prophets live in ascetic hermitages deep in the ice, one of which Genly visits. All the Gethenians he meets have an almost Buddhist acceptance of karma. It even filters down to the level of Le Guin's imagery, which is always concise and economical, and always effective. A Karhide town has houses with 'roofs pitched steep as praying hands' (*Left Hand*, p. 101). This is a fine image, both practical – the roofs are built that way so as not to accumulate snow during the heavy winter storms – and symbolic, a relation of the immanent Gethenian spirituality. This, it seems to me, is why *The Left Hand of Darkness* is set in the landscape it occupies: barrenness is the appropriate environment for spirituality, because it focuses attention on the spirit rather than on the body. And by the same token, Le Guin's genderless world points in the same direction, and prompts us to the same conclusion: that without the sexual distractions of gender, always referring us back to our corporeality, we too could acquire a more spiritual outlook on life.

4

RACE

Race is a key concern of a great deal of contemporary SF, and I
think the reason for this is that twentieth-century science fiction
has been mostly (although clearly not exclusively) an American
phenomenon – produced and consumed in America, or, if not,
then at least heavily influenced by American SF – and race has
been one of the most important cultural and social debates in
postwar American life. It is not surprising that SF, a genre
devoted to the encounter with difference, should have so often
dramatised the various encounters of racial difference that have
done so much to shape contemporary American culture, from the
civil rights movements of the 1960s and the explosion of black
cultural expression of the 1960s and 1970s, through the racial
tension of the 1980s.

It is, however, more than a simple matter of coding 'the alien'
as black, although it sometimes is this. One of the strengths of
science fiction is that it allows for a more complex and sophisticated response to the dynamics of difference, as well as allowing
these issues to be addressed in a popular idiom. This chapter sets
out to discuss aspects of the representation of blackness in SF,
although this is more than merely a matter of identifying black

characters in SF novels. Having a black protagonist may be central to what a novel is trying to do, as in Octavia Butler's superb, if harrowing, *Kindred* (1979); or it may be a purely incidental feature, something not rendered in terms of racial difference at all, or dropped casually into the novel to suggest how far removed its future-world is from the divisions of racial disharmony today – for instance, the protagonist of Robert Heinlein's *Starship Troopers* (1959) is black, although little is made of this feature in the book. Altering the racial identity of the hero in Verhoeven's 1997 film of the book went some way towards producing a more straightforwardly fascist text. This is not the point. The encounter with racial difference, and the profound impact of the black diaspora, has shaped twentieth-century American culture. SF reflects this impact, something it cannot do simply by playing around with protagonists' skin colours. Rendering the diversity of these mutual encounters in their beauty and possibility as well as their violence and bigotry requires a more complex fictive response.

This chapter will look at some of the ways 'blackness' has signified in SF, by looking at two highly regarded authors who are black, Samuel Delany and Octavia Butler, as well as the ways SF has influenced other aspects of black and general popular culture. Various texts have used 'space alien' or 'robot' as a straightforward coding for blackness, but the more interesting representations make complex what can be a straightforward demonisation. Ridley Scott's *Alien* (1979) represents the alien as a black-skinned monster – played, in the original film, by a black actor in a suit – who lurks in the bowels of the industrial ship, a symbol of the industrial city, killing via a ghastly combination of rape and violence. It doesn't take much cultural decoding to see this as an expression of white middle-class fear at the potential for distrust of an alienated black urban underclass. In John McTiernan's *Predator* (1987), the savage hunter alien has dreadlocks, a clear enough signifier of blackness. He inhabits the jungle, preying violently and barbarically on the 'Western' colonisers, be they American, 'Dutch' or Hispanic. He also, when he finally uncovers his face at the end of the movie, has a peculiar mouth with teeth that look like bones pierced through his face – another 'jungle man' caricature of racial blackness. The coding is made even more explicit in the sequel, when the action relocates from the jungle to the urban battlefield of Los Angeles, another, more politically loaded location for white fears of black violence, with the alien joining in the gang war. In the first film, the Predator is destroyed by the Aryan *übermann* Arnold Schwarzenegger. In the second, the casting is even more ingenious: the black actor Danny Glover is pitted against the black-man-as-alien, precisely in the scene where black-on-black violence in contemporary America is at its most acute.

But the SF embodiment of 'black man or woman as alien' need not be as crude as this. For a great many writers, not least black SF authors, exploring the life of the alien becomes a supple and effective way of extrapolating their own positions as alienated individuals. This is the point that Marleen Barr makes when she points out that 'women – especially black women – who are alien in relation to patriarchal society, alter fiction's depiction of the alien' (Barr 1987: 98). Barr's own example – Octavia Butler's *Xenogenesis* trilogy – manages to create alien species that are genuine in their otherness without reducing them to the discourse of violent threat, although Butler is very precise when it comes to delineating the human terror and violence in the face of the radically strange. But there are many other examples of works that detail otherness in a fertile conjunction with blackness, that do so with subtlety and suggestiveness, and in a popular idiom. This chapter ends with a more detailed reading of one such – Barry Sonnenfeld's well-liked and successful film *Men in Black* (1997).

REPRESENTING RACE

Representing blackness, then, is not simply a question of representing black characters or black protagonists in SF texts; not even of representing black characters as empowered, attractive and suchlike. If such representation is not contextualised politically then it can be something incidental, something not to do with the encounter with difference in any meaningful way. I mentioned Heinlein's black protagonist in *Starship Troopers*; we might also point to the protagonist of Ursula Le Guin's *The Left Hand of Darkness*. Genly Ai is a black man, a fact mentioned, by the way, as being unimportant in itself during the course of the fiction. However subtle and sophisticated Le Guin's novel is when it comes to questions of gender difference, racial difference is simply obscured in this novel. Michael Moorcock cast a black man as the central character in his 'Jerry Cornelius' novels (1965–77), but the point of such a racial identity was rather lost in the psychedelic swirl of the 1960s surrealism of those books – unless the point of Jerry's being black was exactly to add an exotic, bohemian edge to the novels, in which case 'blackness' was being deployed in a rather crude, even stereotypical manner (if we think of black as 'different', we need to ask ourselves, 'different to whom?' Difference is a matter of perspective). 'Black' does not connote 'exotic, bohemian otherness' if you happen to be black and brought up in a black environment. More edged is Moorcock's representation of the charismatic black dictator who conquers America in his novel *The Land Leviathan* (1974). As a dictator, Hood commits crimes of oppression and war particularly against whites, but he is always articulate and intelligent when talking about his actions and his motivations, and the novel presents him as paradoxical, never endorsing his violence but never condemning him outright either, aware of the centuries of violence against blacks that constitute American history, against which Hood is only reacting. *The Land Leviathan* is less of a novel than any of the

'Jerry Cornelius' books (it is perfunctory in conception, short, baldly written), but as a text about race it at least avoids presenting race as a hidden issue, something hardly worth talking about.

Samuel Delany, himself a black SF writer and critic, has made a similar point when asked to comment on the Rastafarian characters in William Gibson's celebrated *Neuromancer* (1984). Some critics have seen Gibson's Rastas as a positive racial representation that reflects well on the novel as a whole – a novel, we might argue, that is particularly aware of the varieties of difference. The Rastas live in a jury-rigged orbital colony where they can follow their religion, and their music, in peace; they keep themselves to themselves, although they are not averse to helping Case and his colleagues in their campaign against the international capitalist edifice of Tessier-Ashpool – a positive representation, we might think, of strong, ideologically sound, self-reliant otherness. Delany sees it differently. However much he admires the novel as a whole, he sees Gibson's Rastas as too passive to dramatise the tensions of racial difference effectively; they are 'computer illiterates', 'women are not part of the rasta colony at all', they are presented as being easily manipulated by the sinister Artificial Intelligence, Wintermute. 'As a black reader', he has said, he finds it difficult to applaud 'this passing representation of a powerless and wholly non-oppositional set of black dropouts by a Virginia-born white writer' (Delany in Dery 1993: 751). By way of contrast, Delany cites a very different text, Robert Heinlein's *Farnham's Freehold* (1964). In that novel, a black manservant called Joseph abandons, after a nuclear attack, the white family he has served. Postnuclear America faces famine, and Joseph becomes the leader of a black group whose solution to this problem is to go around killing and eating whites. It might seem, on the surface, that this unpleasant story is nothing short of racist. Heinlein, after all, was as well known for his sometimes extreme right-wing views as for his influential SF, and this novel might be thought of as dramatising middle-class white anxieties about the American black underclass ('if we give them the chance, they'll turn on us and devour us'). But Delany insists that, because this is a novel that dramatises racial difference in terms of conflict, because its very extremism makes us think, it functions as a better book 'about' race:

> Though I doubt that [many readers] would approve of the course or outcome of Heinlein's story, the point is that Joseph is articulate, he has real power, and Heinlein is consciously ironizing powerful cultural myths of cannibalism precisely for their troubling anxieties. He forces us, in the course of his tale, to think through the situation – even if we don't agree with him, or his mouthpiece, Hugh Farnham.
>
> (Delany in Dery 1993: 752)

For Delany the moral seems to be that an SF novel needs to aim not at political correctness, or at an unspoken decency regarding race; instead it should make us think about these issues, confront us with them, as only a literature of ideas can. Certainly, Delany's own work has been fascinated with the complex interactions between cultures and races from the beginning. One of his most famous novels, *The Einstein Intersection* (1968), is a brief but immensely fertile and suggestive fable on the workings of difference. As Damien Broderick puts it, 'from his earliest fictions...Samuel Delany has followed the vocation of what we might call "allographer", one who writes the Other' (Broderick 1995: 117).

In *The Einstein Intersection*, Earth has been abandoned long ago by humanity, and is now inhabited by a diverse range of mutated and exotic variations on the old 'human' model. Some of these mutations have produced striking and positive changes – from characters who can read minds or see the future to those who have increased strength and dexterity. At the other end of the scale, some mutations are so debilitating and deforming that those born with them must be sequestered, put in the 'kage'. As the protagonist, Lo Lobey (the 'Lo' as a forename signifies his masculinity, just as 'La' before a name signifies femaleness and 'Le' androgyny), travels from the countryside to the city we realise that these posthumans are acting out the primal myths of their human predecessors – living in the ruins, as it were, of human culture. As one character puts it, 'we have taken over their abandoned world, and something new is happening to the fragments, something we can't even define with mankind's leftover vocabulary' (p. 131). Lo Lobey's story might be defined as a version of the ancient myth of Orpheus and Eurydice, or the myth of Theseus and the Minotaur, or the more contemporary (to us) myth of Billy the Kid, but none of these narrative templates are adequate to describe what happens in this poetic, exotic, strange and beautiful little book. Indeed this is Delany's whole point, that 'difference' is not something that can be completely apprehended by the vocabulary of sameness, that there is always going to be something beyond, which can't be expressed in the old language. This is why the tutelary spirit of the novel, as it were, is the twentieth-century mathematician Godel; the place where his Incompleteness theorem (of which the novel provides an artistic embodiment) intersects with the more rationalist Einsteinian physics provides the novel's title. 'Different' is a term that crops up again and again in the novel; it is the word used by characters to denote 'mutated', 'changed', 'possessing some ability that is outwith the range of the normal'. When Lobey reveals that he can read a character's mind, that character asks 'you're different, aren't you?' (p. 75). But it is also used negatively, as a shorthand for the bigoted dismissal of otherness. In these terms, 'different' means merely 'freak' or 'deformed'. The positive and the negative deployment of the discourse of difference, of course, has its resonances with the debates about 'race' that have been so prominent in twentieth-century America.

Difference for Delany, it needs to be stressed, is about more than just race. In this novel, for instance, it becomes an almost universal artistic enabler, a means of opening up possibilities. But we can't ignore the fact that difference in Delany's hands is *also* about race. Lobey, for instance, introduces himself in self-deprecating terms that inevitably enter the discourse of race.

> What do I look like?
>
> Ugly and grinning most of the time. That's a whole lot of big nose and gray eyes and wide mouth crammed on a small brown face proper for a fox...I have a figure like a bowling pin, thighs, calves, and feet of a man (gorilla?) twice my size (which is about five-nine) and hips to match. There was a rash of hermaphrodites the year I was born, which doctors thought I might be...My feet have toes almost as long as my fingers, and the big ones are semi-opposable.
>
> (Delany, *Einstein Intersection* (1970): 7–8)

Delany is self-consciously playing with negative racial stereotypes here, and going some way towards reversing their associations. Lobey is a musician; he has a hollow machete with holes down the blade: 'when I blow across the mouthpiece in the handle, I make music with my blade' (p. 1). Or to put it another way, he is an artist, like Delany himself. That Lobey is gorilla-like, in the terms of this novel, means only that he has a greater dexterity – he can, for instance, play his iconic musical flute-sword with his fingers or his toes – as well as greater strength. Delany also deliberately contrasts a certain rustic crudity (Lobey) with the suave deadliness of the racially white Kid Death, with his red hair and white skin ('his skin', says one character, 'was soap white').

Delany effectively introduces himself into the novel via Lobey (a self-referential cypher) as well as quoting extensively from his own authorial journals as chapter epigraphs. And there is a racial reason why it is Lobey who destroys Kid Death at the novel's end and not the other way around. In Delany's universe it is diversity and hybridity that are strength. 'To survive even a dozen more generations,' says the novel's Jean Harlow/Aphrodite figure, 'we must keep the genes mixing, mixing, mixing' (p. 146). Delany's own racially mixed heritage, his own diversely focused sexuality, his varied life and eclectic literary tastes all come together to produce him as an artist and to produce his art; and this is something he puts unambiguously into his novel. Lobey is not just different because of a few physical markers to do with his skin and physiognomy (which is to say, different racially); his difference is something more profound. A random mutation has given him the ability to hear the music in other people's minds and to recreate it on his musical sword – has made him, in other words, an artist. Kid Death is contemptuous of this ability:

> 'What power do you have?' Kid Death demanded. 'What can you do with your difference! Speak to a few deaf men, dead men, pierce the minds of a few idiots?'
>
> (Delany, *Einstein Intersection* (1970): 106)

But the force and beauty of this novel take its brown-skinned protagonist on a quest towards the core of what Art is, a quest that results in the destruction of Kid Death.

As a means of reclaiming 'difference' as a positive quantity, SF has provided many black writers and artists with the means to reconfigure prejudice. Nor is this confined to printed media. Kodwo Eshun's book *More Brilliant Than the Sun* (1998) has explored the black component of what he calls 'sonic fiction' – the ways popular music has taken on the tropes and trappings of SF to express itself. The first rock star to fully explore SF was probably David Bowie; his 'Major Tom' character, followed by his *Stationtostation* persona as 'The Man Who Fell To Earth', found in SF an effortlessly effective carriage for the gender-bending otherworldly weirdness. 'Difference' here is predominantly gender, and fits neatly into an imagined SF universe. But, as Eshun demonstrates, there were a great many black musicians drawn to the same fantastic strategies for locating their own notions of 'difference'. George Clinton and Funkadelic (for instance) employ the vocabulary of space travel and the 'mothership' as a means of articulating racial difference in a positive manner; and more recently Tricky and Goldie have matched the futuristic timbre of their techno-music with the iconography of SF. As Eshun suggests, part of the point of these sorts of artistic endeavour has been to distance black art from stereotypes. In music, the most enduring of these stereotypes has been 'the Street', the sense that black music comes from and therefore necessarily must reflect a certain range of gritty urban realities. Refusing to conform to this caricature, and instead conceptualising black music as expansively fantastic, becomes a powerful artistic manoeuvre. Representation does not need to be chained to a limited notion of 'realism' to have powerful, realistic effects. Art can create a climate where the first associations of blackness are not 'Huggy Bear' (the shady black underworld character from *Starsky and Hutch*), but rather Geordi LaForge or Guinan from the starship *Enterprise*.

RACE AND *STAR TREK*

A recent (1996) book by Mia Consalio has anatomised *Star Trek* on grounds of race, and finds the show limited and even tacitly racist. In some senses, *Trek* might seem an odd target for anti-racist wrath. Gene Roddenberry was vocal about his desire to represent a future in which discrimination on grounds of race or gender was a thing of the past, and was proud of the ethnically integrated bridge crew, with a white American captain, Japanese and Russian helm officers, a black woman communications officer and so on. But as Consalio points out, the apparent diversity of the crew was in fact subordinated to the white ideal represented by Kirk; Lieutenant Uhura (whose dialogue was often extremely limited, and sometimes pared down to 'hailing frequencies open,

Captain') was a marginal figure in many senses. The idea here is that the original series of *Star Trek* was a text of its time, and that representation of race was predicated upon a sense that 'whiteness' was the norm, from which other races deviated (and to which other races might aspire). Supporters of the show point to its consistently applied liberal ethos, and the fact that many episodes directly addressed issues of race and racial discrimination. 'Let That Be Your Last Battlefield' is one example of this. Kirk and the crew come across a planet caught in a savage civil war between two different 'races'. The people of this planet are humanoid, and divided into two colours by a line running down the middle of their faces and bodies (a rather harlequinesque colour scheme), with one side black and the other white. One portion of the population is black on the left side and white on the right; the other section is *white* on the left side and *black* on the right. Their mutual hatred strikes us as based on an especially arbitrary discrimination, and the message of the show – that racial conflict in our own time is similarly arbitrary – is unmistakable. Indeed, this show is rather clever: the device is so egregious, the whole show is so patently predicated upon one straightforward liberal point, that it tacitly encourages the viewer to go beyond the parameters of the text – to say, in effect, 'of course such racism (and by extension, any racism) is absurd, but I wonder about the particulars of culture and tradition that might separate these two peoples', and so on. Liberal fans of *Star Trek* might also point out that it often represented black characters in senior social positions (renowned doctors, senior officers), and that it was the first show on American TV to show an inter-racial kiss – between Kirk and Uhura. But this kiss is not actually as straightforwardly a blow for racial equality as it sounds. Although Kirk seems to spend almost every episode kissing one or other (white-skinned, or in one case green-skinned) alien – so much so that a rather troglodyte version of 'command masculinity' is constructed by the show – his single kiss with a black-skinned woman is a fraught affair. He does not *want* to kiss Uhura, perhaps because she is one of his crew (although he has no problem desiring white-skinned members of his crew in other episodes), and she does not want to kiss him. They are both compelled to kiss by evil, mind-controlling aliens, who force this degrading and 'wrong' spectacle for their own entertainment. Overall, it is difficult to deny that 'blackness' in the original series of *Star Trek* is a marginalised quantity, and that 'whiteness' is not only normalised but represented as an ideal.

Mia Consalio goes on to criticise *Star Trek: the Next Generation* on similar grounds, but this I think ignores the increasing presence of 'blackness' in American SF. To quote Consalio:

> Lieutenant Worf [played by black actor Michael Dorn] is the first Klingon to serve on a Starfleet vessel and is a prominent member of the cast, given feature episodes and many scenes. However, racist beliefs about African-Americans give the figure of Worf, as well as all Klingons, stereotypical traits that mark them as unlike or not quite equal to the white 'ideal'. For example, the Klingons are portrayed as an extremely warlike race, given to strong emotion and physical displays of strength and power. This is in contrast to the more sedate, presumably superior traits of Captain Jean-Luc Picard (a Frenchman with an English accent), who is famous for his diplomatic skills as well as his intelligence and control.
>
> (Consalio 1996: 544)

This, I think, fails to do justice to the increasing sensitivity of the *Star Trek* franchise to issues of colour. One of the main characters in *The Next Generation* – Geordi – is played by LeVar Burton, another black actor. Burton played the character of Kunta Kinte in the extremely popular TV dramatisation of Alex Haley's *Roots* (1976), a show which constituted pretty much the first time many of the issues of racial discrimination and the appalling history of slavery were given an airing on national TV. Burton acquired a significant fan-base amongst African-Americans (and others) on the back of this groundbreaking portrayal, and his decision to play Geordi in *Trek* took many of these fans with him. What seems to me to be positive about Burton's portrayal of Geordi is the way it resolutely refuses the stereotypical attributes of black manhood – Geordi is, basically, a supercompetent computer nerd, not a type usually represented by black characters. In the show, and especially in the early series, Geordi is extremely dedicated to his work, shy around women, with relatively poor social skills, and his best friend is a robot. He is also blind, a feature which occasionally elicits negative discrimination from others (as in the episode 'The Masterpiece Society'), although his skin colour never does. He is also, I should add, a very appealing character, a senior officer with real powers and responsibilities, and is given a great many feature episodes and important scenes. It is this sort of complex casting both with and against type that marks out a certain sophistication in *Trek*'s representation of colour.

The Klingons make an interesting case study in the representation of 'race'. In the original series they were played by white actors and seemed, fairly straightforwardly, to connote 'Orientalism', particularly a caricature of the Japanese. Their faces, hair and samurai costumes as much as their warrior society were particularly suggestive in America in the 1960s, a time when many Americans (Roddenberry included) had fresh memories of fighting the Japanese in the Second World War. As they appear in the original series, the Klingons are without redeeming qualities: they are brutish, devious, dangerous and murderous, the very embodiment of a racist demonisation of the oriental other. But for the cinematic adventures of the *Star Trek* crew, and then in *Star Trek: the Next Generation*, the Klingons are treated in a more sympathetic light. Although still violent and aggressive, the presence of Worf on the *Enterprise*, followed by a large number of episodes set amongst Klingon culture, fleshed out their way of life, making it seem much more attractive. Fans loved it, and a wide range of spin-offs from the series entered general circulation – the Klingon language, for instance, was invented fully enough for people to converse in it, and Klingon dictionaries and grammatical primers sold well. CD-ROMS giving more insight into the Klingon way were also popular, and as first *Star Trek: the Next Generation* and then *Star Trek: Deep Space Nine* devoted more time to Klingon characters and concerns, it became apparent that a race introduced in the original series as the Villains had become the Heroes.

This shift from villain status to hero status is marked, I think, by a revealing shift in the cultural sensibilities with which Klingons are apprehended. In short, this involves an internalisation of the cultural signifier 'Klingon' into a North American cultural logic, albeit one that still marks their separation. What I mean by this is that, from being coded as 'Japanese' (and therefore un-American), the Klingons became coded as African-American (almost all Klingon characters are now played by African-American actors), and more specifically as Native-American (the 'warrior culture' integral to Klingon life became less samurai and more Sioux: so that, for instance, the Klingon war-cry, 'Today is a good day to die!', is drawn from Sioux traditions). Whilst neither African-American nor Native-American represent the dominant cultural strand in current constructions of 'American-ness', they are both potent and significant narratives within that overall ideology. Villain (equal to 'un-American') had been made American as part of the process of recreating the Klingons as heroic.

At the time of writing, the dominant *Star Trek* franchise is *Star Trek: Deep Space Nine*, a show set on a space station where a black captain, Sisko, presides over a crew with a wide range of black and ethnic characters (including Michael Dorn's Worf, transferred from the *Enterprise*). Although the bulk of the programme makes no reference to the main character's skin colour, *DS9* is a show unafraid to deal directly with the reality of racism: in one episode, Sisko is propelled back in time to 1950s Earth, where he becomes a science-fiction writer. There he encounters racial discrimination, something unknown in the twenty-fifth century, and something that is put over in a shocking and disturbing fashion.

Star Trek's approach to the questions of race, then, is not exactly utopian; but it does at least allow a space for debate, a significant role for black actors and characters and a certain utopian impulse that encourages viewers to think *through* problems of difference.

ALIEN ABDUCTION

Race, I have been suggesting, is something central to late twentieth-century constructions of 'American-ness'; and I have also been saying that SF is one of the most characteristic of expressions of American culture. It doesn't surprise me, then, that race is so ubiquitous in American SF. This reveals itself, not just in novels written from an SF perspective, but also in culture in general.

The argument would go something like this: because race has been so important to postwar America, the myths and discourses of America tend to embody a consciousness of race. What, for instance, primarily distinguishes 'the space alien' from the human being? We might say any number of things (tentacles, bug-eyes, many arms, slime and so on), but the chances are we would agree on one thing: skin colour. Aliens, as popular consciousness knows, are differently coloured – green-skinned, blue-skinned, or (more latterly) grey-skinned. Skin colour, in other words, is reflected by SF as the key vector of difference. TV shows such as *Alien Nation* (which was a spin-off from a popular film) posit the arrival of aliens from another world who settle amongst humanity to live and work like any other immigrants as the underclass of affluent America. Apart from a number of bizarre differences (the ability to get drunk on sour milk, being burnt by seawater as if by acid, and so on) the predominant difference between humans and these humanoid aliens is their skin colour (the aliens are patterned exotically – we might almost say in jungle colours). As SF writer Greg Tate points out, in *Alien Nation* the aliens 'were former slaves who were brought to earth on a ship and just dumped on these shores' (Tate, in Dery 1993: 764). It seems almost too straightforward an SF allegory.

A show such as *The X-Files*, on the other hand, has little explicitly to say about race. But its dominant narrative fascination – alien abduction – is a revealing contemporary American myth. Studies put the number of Americans who literally believe in alien abduction in the millions, and a variety of critics have attempted to come to terms with why this story is so extraordinarily popular (see, for instance, Luckhurst 1998). One thing the alien abduction narrative does, as several black critics have noted, is to retell the story of the African slave trade by relocating it to a contemporary SF context. The typical abductee is a white, moderately affluent thirty-something American. Abductees are taken suddenly from their homes by aliens, restrained (perhaps shackled) and transported to the alien spaceship. Once there they are subjected to physically degrading and sometimes painful treatment by aliens who seem callously indifferent to their suffering. Some of these treatments seem to involve some sort of 'tagging' (the insertion, for instance, of devices into nose or ear); some of them constitute sexual assault (the insertion of probes into genital or rectal areas, the stimulation of the penis and the removal of sperm, or the investigation of the womb). At the end of this process, the aliens compel the abductees to forget, or at least to suppress, memories of the experience, usually with some quasi-telepathic invasion of the mind. What happens with alien abduction, in other words, is what Freudians call 'the return of the repressed', although on a societal level. The brutal realities of the trade in slaves (the abduction of people from their homes, the physical humiliation and violence, the sexual assault) are intimately complicit with the history and indeed the success of America. Such narratives sit uncomfortably with the discourse of 'the land of the free', and have been largely (and, until recently, successfully) suppressed, to be replaced with stories of Pilgrim Fathers and intrepid wagon trains going west. But things do not disappear by being pushed down into the political unconscious, and the return of this violent, cruel and fundamentally American narrative manifests itself in a variety of new ways. In the case of alien abduction, mainstream America is fantasising a science-fictionalised version of eighteenth- and nineteenth-century slaving, and interpolating itself into the victim role. It is very much to do with race.

One of today's most highly regarded novelists, Octavia Butler, takes the alien abduction narrative as the starting point for her masterpiece, the *Xenogenesis* trilogy. In the first novel of this trilogy, *Dawn* (1987), Lilith Iyapo, a well-to-do African-American woman, wakes to find herself in a grey, enclosed room aboard a spaceship. She has no memory of how she came to be there, and cannot explain the scar across her belly, something which seems to suggest invasive alien procedures. Interrogation by her alien captors is, in the first instance, an intimidating and sinister business: 'Her captors spoke when they were ready and not before. They did not show themselves at all. She remained sealed in her cubicle and their voices came to her from above like the light' (Butler, *Dawn* (1997): 5). Lilith remembers the nuclear war that had destroyed her world, and remembers the death of her family.

As the novel continues, the aliens reveal themselves not to be malicious or sadistic, but instead benign and positive. They have rescued the remnants of humanity from the aftermath of nuclear conflict and have kept them unconscious on their orbiting spaceship for 250 years, until the Earth could be made habitable again. They intend to awaken this human population and release it back into the wild, as it were. In return they require only one thing from humanity: their genes. Butler's aliens, the Oankali, are essentially traders in genetic material, continually augmenting their own bodies with genetic diversity from other species, a process they can control at a molecular level. These aliens, then, are the symbolic embodiment of diversity; and their strength – the technology they wield (which is always represented in suitably Edenic, utopian manner, as *organic* technology), their position as the literal saviours of mankind, and their uniformly rational, kindly demeanour – reflects that diversity as a fundamental good. Diversity and hybridity are the absolute raison-d'être of these aliens: 'we do what you would call genetic engineering', one of them tells Lilith. 'We do it naturally. We *must* do it. It renews us, enables us to survive as an evolving species instead of specialising ourselves into extinction or stagnation' (p. 39). As a result of this, Butler's Oankali have a radically contrary approach to Difference to that of most humans. In the second book of the trilogy, Lilith says as much, talking to her son, a hybrid human-Oankali called Akin:

> 'Human beings fear difference,' Lilith had told him once. 'Oankali crave difference. Humans persecute their different ones, yet they need them to give themselves definition and status. Oankali seek difference and collect it. They need it to keep themselves from stagnation and overspecialisation...When you feel a conflict [within yourself], try to go the Oankali way. Embrace difference.'
>
> (Butler, *Adulthood Rites* (1997): 80)

That last sentence might stand as the epigraph for the whole *Xenogenesis* trilogy. It is interesting to contrast the Oankali – a race of aliens who cruise the galaxy seeking out new life in order to assimilate its difference to themselves, and who are not prepared to leave any unaltered human beings behind on earth – with a similarly conceived race of aliens from *Star Trek*, the Borg. The Borg are thoroughly evil, conceived only in terms of threat, the most extreme of *Trek*'s demonisations of the alien as other. Butler's Oankali, on the other hand, constitute one of SF's most convincing utopian experiments, a profound and moving exploration of the possibilities alterity could bring with it.

This attempt at utopia is one strand of Butler's trilogy; but perhaps the books are more focused on the extreme difficulty all the humans have in the face of such radical difference. In the first volume, Lilith undergoes a slow and painful process of acclimatisation to the strangeness of the aliens. Their skin, which is covered in sensory tentacles and feelers of varying sizes ('Medusa children. Snakes for hair. Nests of night crawlers for eyes and ears'), causes her the most problem (*Dawn*, p. 41). Even when she accepts the aliens, and even takes an alien mate, the sheer weirdness of these phallic organs continues to bother her. That there is something sexual at the root of this *unheimlich* quality is made explicit both in their characterisation, and by the fact that Lilith and her human partner find a super-sexual bliss in conjunction with their mutual alien mate:

> She tore off her jacket and seized the ugly, ugly elephant's trunk of an organ, letting it coil round her as she climbed onto the bed. She sandwiched Nikanj's [the alien's] body between her own and Joseph's.
>
> (Butler, *Dawn* (1997): 161)

But it is the setting of a black woman at the core of this story that brings us back to issues of race. We discover that Lilith has been awakened by the Oankali for a particular reason: she is to 'parent' a group of newly-awakened humans, to guide them into a position of acceptance of their new position. She doesn't want this job, but that is the very reason why she has been given it by the aliens: 'somebody who desperately doesn't want the responsibility, who doesn't want to lead, who is a woman' (*Dawn*, p. 157). In other words, as Jenny Wolmark puts it, this is a novel about the ways a character's 'marginality, articulated in terms of both gender and race, [can] become her strength' (Wolmark 1994: 32). As a black woman, Lilith might traditionally be represented as marginal; but Butler's SF context redefines the concept of the marginal with the hybrid space aliens in whose domain the story takes place.

CASE STUDY: BLACKNESS IN SONNENFELD'S *MEN IN BLACK* (1997)

Barry Sonnenfeld's 1997 film *Men in Black* is currently (2000) Columbia Picture's biggest-earning movie; and the range of its success in cinemas, and latterly on video, is at least in part an index of the ways it is able to encapsulate certain contemporary concerns. What I want to do with the rest of this chapter is talk about the resonances of the 'black' of the title. Partly this has to do with a certain code of clothing, something that connects with the economy of 'cool' that has given the movie its cachet; partly I want to argue that *Men in Black* is a text about race in America.

That this is a movie that encodes a certain text about race is, perhaps, on reflection an obvious observation. I have already rehearsed in this chapter the familiar-enough arguments that a dominant feature of American science fiction, and SF cinema in particular, has been an encoding of the black man as alarming alien in films such as *Alien* and *Predator*. Aliens exist as a marginal quantity in conventional 'American Dream' ideology, as an unnamed and external other, sometimes benign (as in Spielberg's ET, the alien who embodies certain qualities, the voodoo/spiritual and childlike qualities, of the white cultural representation of blackness), but more usually threatening and violent. There have been many studies of the ways in which American culture has represented blackness as other, of course;

and the alien as black is, in a sense, simply an extension of this idea. But it is the potency of the SF imaginative space, what it means to the continuation of the frontier ideology of the American renaissance, that gives this particular marginalisation of difference to otherness, usually threatening otherness, its particular bite.

Men in Black, then, is explicitly about the immigrant experience. The premise of the film is that space aliens are among us already, disguised as human beings. The secret 'Men in Black' organisation has been set up, apparently extra-governmentally (using money gleaned from the careful exploitation of alien technology in the form of microwave ovens, computers and suchlike), to monitor these immigrants. These incomers are treated exactly like previous waves of US immigration (which is to say, they are not regarded as being any more out-of-the-ordinary than any previous historical wave of immigration), although they are more heavily monitored (from a high-tech bank of computer screens) and their movement is restricted. They are, then, internalised outsiders, aliens in disguise, and as such they represent a danger to the body politic, a danger that it is the job of the 'Men in Black' to keep under control. What this danger precisely is (over and above the mere exposure of their true natures), or why these aliens wanted to come to Earth in the first place, is not actually spelled out in the movie. What is clear, though, is that the burden of the film represents the immigrant as visually different from the 'normal' American, and as possessing a dangerous potential. There is also an explicitly aligned racial component to the film's premise. Into this context the film builds a second narrative, one that involves the recruitment and training of a new agent in the MiB organisation, played by Will Smith. It is not, I would suggest, a mere incidental detail that this new character is the only black individual in the entire film.

The Will Smith character (Jay) represents something of a departure from the original conception of the movie. In Lowell

Cunningham's originary comic strip 'The Men in Black' (Marvel Comics), upon which the film is based, the two protagonists are both white males. Casting Smith, with a nod towards his success in (say) *Independence Day* and his undoubted box-office draw, may have had little to do with his colour. But, apart from bringing the only black face to the Men in Black (an organisation otherwise exclusively white, at least as represented – with only trivial exception – in the film), Smith also deliberately vocalises issues of race. Donning his Ray-Bans to complete his black suit, white shirt, black tie look, the camera zooms in on his face. 'You know what the difference is between you and me?' he asks one of his colleagues; 'I make this look *good*.' Black men, according to some received wisdom, are more stylish, more 'cool' than white (and Smith does look extremely smart in his black clothes); but if we are going to follow stereotypes then we might also want to explore the ways 'black' is a signifier for, say, urban crime. In an early scene of the film, Smith is chasing after a suspect (who, although Smith doesn't realise it, is actually an alien). As part of the chase, Smith jumps from a bridge and lands in the open upper deck of a tour bus. 'It just be raining black men in New York,' he tells the startled tourists – a line not in the original shooting script, but a neatly appropriate ad-lib. What starts out in the original comic strip as banter about age, with Kay as old and worldweary and Jay as a young tyro, is inflected in the movie by Smith's presence into something also about race. Smith's brand of stand-up jive-talking accelerates this impression. Deciding to be part of the MiB, Jay announces that he's accepting a place in the organisation but that he expects to be treated with respect: 'And I don't want nobody calling me "son" nor "kid" nor "sport" nor nothing like that'. As the film goes on, both Tommy Lee Jones's Kay and Rip Torn's Zee repeatedly refer to Smith with exactly this manner of sobriquet – 'tiger', 'slick', 'scooter', 'ace' and so on. They never actually call him 'boy', it is true, although the shadow of the elderly Southern white Zee calling this young black man 'boy' is never far away. Then again there are the aliases that Kay and Jay use when working in New York. When they visit the house of Edgar's widow (Edgar's body has been taken over by an alien), Kay introduces them both: 'Ma'am, I am Special Agent Mannheim, and this is Special Agent Black.' Later in the morgue, Jay is no longer 'Black' but 'Doctor White'; and later still Kay refers to him as 'Sergeant Friday' (is this, we ask, because he is a sort of Man Friday to Kay's forlorn Robinson Crusoe; or is it a reference to the character Friday from the American TV show *Dragnet*?).

Blackness, in this film, begins then with the blackness of space (the movie's first shot), and goes on to the blackness of the car, the suit, the dark glasses, and finally with the recruitment of Jay to blackness as skin colour. As in Ralph Ellison's famous novel of black experience, *Invisible Man* (1952), this blackness is specifically invoked as the colour of invisibility, anonymity. This is underlined again by the 'Neuralyzer', the light-pen that blots out memory, one of the more memorable gimmicks from the film. The way it is used is to erase knowledge that the aliens are amongst us and that there is this 'black' agency servicing them. Or, more exactly, since the aliens live amongst us and therefore we can't be ignorant of their presence, the pen operates to erase the knowledge of their *difference*. We take these aliens as versions of ourselves, we assimilate them into 'our' (white middle-class) experience, rather than recognising them as other. The space alien as coded black man, in this film, is most significantly characterised as invisible.

A key scene, then, is the dressing scene: the scene in which Will Smith's Jay is given his 'Men in Black' defining suit of clothes. Rip Torn's Zee describes this suit as 'the last suit you'll ever need'. The suit, then, is one of the most obvious, most striking aspects of the film's styling: it provides a uniform that is instantly recognisable. But the point about these clothes is that they are supposed to confer anonymity, which is precisely the point of the Men in Black organisation: we see various shots of Jay being relieved of his fingerprints and having his computer records erased prior to being fitted out, whilst we hear Rip Torn as controller Zee in voice-over:

'You will have no identifying marks of any kind. You will not stand out in any way...anonymity is your name, silence your native speech...You are no longer part of the system. You are above the system, over it, beyond it.'

John Harvey's excellent study of the fashion for black suits down the ages, his like-titled book *Men in Black* (a study published several years before the movie), makes exactly these points about dressing in black. Harvey's study is an attempt to answer the question why, 'in this age of supreme wealth and power [the nineteenth-century], the men who wielded precisely this power and who possessed this wealth wanted to dress as if going to a funeral'. Black suits are curiously double-edged signifiers, as Harvey demonstrates. '[Black] is a colour without colour that speaks loudly because it is conspicuous, even if it says "Don't see me! I efface myself" ' (Harvey 1995: 14). It is for these reasons, Harvey argues, that men of power have gravitated towards black clothes in the nineteenth and twentieth centuries: they wish to avoid the dangerous spotlight of public recognition (something that began at about the time of the French Revolution, when being conspicuous frequently led to the guillotine), whilst simultaneously encoding wealth, power and (according to Harvey) spirituality.

Our outer dress does inner work for us, and if clothes mean anything, it is in the first place to ourselves, telling us we are or may be something we have meant to be...In dressing we enter an inheritance, which may include a new self, which we feel to be a true self, revealed or rather realised by the donning of these good clothes.

(Harvey 1995: 14)

In the film *Men in Black*, Jay enters into exactly such an inheritance by putting on his trademark suit. But the aliens in the film also wear 'suits', although these are of a more fleshly nature. Some, like the Arquillian Emperor, seem to be mechanical contrivances that only look like bodies, but others are actual people, people-as-suits in a comic twist to the plotline of *Silence of the Lambs*. Edgar's widow speaks of her husband, taken over by the Bug, as if 'something was wearing Edgar...like a suit...an Edgar suit' (a phrase Kay later repeats). Similarly, though, there is an appropriateness, the articulation of an inner truth about these respective choices of suit–body. In this sense, *Men in Black* is a film about the ways bodily identity (for instance, and most obviously, racial identity) is performative in precisely the way that clothing identity is.

Harvey's study goes on to explore the connotations of black clothes in a more political light. Some black clothing, he argues, can embody the black 'not only of a nation but rather of an empire':

> For there is certainly a connection between black and empire...it is noticeable...that whenever a European nation as a whole has taken black as its fashion, this has occurred at that nation's greatest moment of international power. This is true of Burgundy in the fifteenth century, of Venice in the fifteenth and sixteenth centuries, of Spain in the sixteenth century, of the Dutch republic in the seventeenth century and of England in the nineteenth century. It is not hard to see how the values of black discussed earlier in this study – self-effacement and uniformity, impersonality and authority, discipline and self-discipline, a willingness to be strict and a willingness to die – might assist in maintaining an imperial order.
>
> (Harvey 1995: 156)

This connects, it seems to me, with the unabashed way in which the film revels (under a certain cloaking of irony and comedy) in the repressive power of these sorts of State Apparatus; the way it glorifies the repressive technologies deployed by the MiB. Early in the film Kay explains the circumstances that have led to so many aliens inhabiting Manhattan. 'Did you ever see the movie *Casablanca?*' he asks. 'It's the same thing, except without the Nazis.' But the Nazis are not, perhaps, so far away. The politically privileged position of the Men in Black (over the system, beyond it) is never subjected to critique (of course not, we might think: this is a comedy). And yet humanity in this film is consistently represented as insignificant, puerile, idiotic, despicable. 'Pond scum', Edgar calls us; whilst our self-appointed protector, Kay, reveals that 'human thought is so primitive it is regarded as an infectious disease in some of the better galaxies'. Jay, before recruitment, wonders if it wouldn't be better actually to tell people what is going on, on the grounds that, being smart, they can cope with it. But Kay contradicts him. 'A person is smart,' he says. 'People are dumb, panicky, dangerous animals, and you know it.' From this perspective, the film becomes a rather unsettling glorification of a secret service self-avowedly not dedicated to the good of the people. At its white, male core, the Men in Black organisation has its surveillance mechanism, a room with a giant TV screen which can be used to focus on anything – and anyone – in the entire world (Kay, for instance, uses it to spy on his long-lost lover). 'Observation,' as Zee describes it; 'the heart of our little endeavour.' What this 'observation' amounts to is a high-tech version of Foucault's panopticon (the penitentiary designed by Jeremy Bentham in which one person seated in the middle can observe all the inmates simultaneously, which Foucault saw as an emblem of the repressive aspect of modern life). This technology is legitimised because it is only to be used to spy on aliens; but none the less it is a pretty spooky thing, and it is spooky exactly because this particular high-tech panopticon, with its octopus-armed alien secretarial assistants, is such a *cool* device; or is unambiguously represented as such in the film. The MiB are cool-looking, and they have a whole bunch of cool technology – cool even though all of it (the 'Neuralyzer', the panopticon, the weaponry) is used against *us*.

Of course, it could easily be argued that I am perpetrating some sort of category error by reading a lighthearted comedy in these terms (we could make a similar argument about the valorisation of repressive state apparatuses in Cameron's *True Lies* – also a comedy). I am not trying to avoid the fact that *Men in Black* is funny; nor that its humour is the same strain of black humour that Sonnenfeld honed during his time as cinematographer to the Coen brothers, or in his own directorial *The Addams Family* and *Addams Family Values* movies. Perhaps I can best bring my argument to a close with reference to a different sort of theoretical perspective: Kristeva, of *Powers of Horror* (1982). This might seem a strange move, but in one sense there can be little doubt that this is a film engaged in the cinematic representation of abjection. It is far from unusual in this respect, of course: contemporary SF and horror cinema has reached astonishing heights of special effects verisimilitude in the representation of all manner of slime, puss, goo, vomit, shit, scum and visceral unmentionables. The cinema audiences' appetite for such revolting stuff never ceases to amaze. We could take a representative text (John Carpenter's *The Thing*, for instance) and look at the way such movie abjection plays a crucial part in the aesthetics of this particular genre. But we don't need to, because *Men in Black* is as abject a film as any. It begins with a bug squashed, up close, on a truck windscreen; and moves on to 'Mikey', a green-skinned alien masquerading as an illegal immigrant trying to enter the USA from Mexico (a none-too-subtle reference to the race encoding of the movie as a whole). When 'Mikey' runs at a highway patrolman, Kay shoots him to pieces with a ray-gun, showering the policeman in unspeakable filth ('Looks like you got some entrails on you there, pal'). The film moves on through a variety of such revolting scenes: Jay helps another alien give birth, only to have the cute-eyed alien baby puke all over him; Edgar, the Bug alien, kills the porter at the morgue by sticking him to the ceiling with bug-goo; and in the climactic scene, Kay climbs into the intestinal tract of the Bug (now freed from his human 'suit' and grown to an enormous size) to retrieve his gun – shooting his way free, and showering bits and pieces of space-cockroach gloop everywhere.

The pleasure we receive in watching all this abject matter is of a curious sort. As I understand it, Kristeva sees abjection in material that is not exactly of us, and yet not exactly clearly attributable to a well-defined otherness. Not us, not not-us, but blurring the borderline between the two. This is the position of the Men in Black themselves, when considered socially. They belong to an organisation outside normal society, even outside government (they don't answer to government: who 'ask too many questions'); in a sense they have become abject from society itself. And the slimy aliens, in their multicoloured (never black) human suits, exist uneasily on this borderline, partly of humanity, partly and obviously not so. And in a final twist, the Men in Black themselves, sandwiched between the 'pond scum' of humanity and the revolting cockroach abjection of the alien, are themselves abjected from abjection. This abject matter can be any colour, but it cannot be black: and whilst actress Linda Fiorentino's dress is messed and dirtied during her abduction by the Bug, the black suits of Kay and Jay, filthy with slime in one shot, are miraculously clean in the next. These Suits of Power, then, represent a particular sort of political and personal potency, a magic invisibility/celebrity, a transformation of black America's most powerful cultural capital – Cool – into a quasi-political, organisational and technological reality.

5

TECHNOLOGY AND METAPHOR

Machines and technology are what we most associate with SF; just as we have now grown utterly accustomed to having a wide range of machines and technology surrounding us in our everyday lives. This might make it difficult for 'the machine' to figure alterity; but there can be little doubt that this is precisely the space occupied by the machine in the SF text.

We might think of high-tech machines as the necessary props of any SF tale. A novel may be in every salient regard a straightforward realist novel, but this straightforward realist content set on a spaceship travelling between the stars becomes Science Fiction. C J Cherryh's *Port Eternity* (1982) retells the legends of King Arthur aboard a spaceship with robots playing the roles of knights and ladies: these two nova, the spaceship and the robot, are what relocates the story from Arthurian fantasy to SF. James Cameron's *Terminator* (1984) is Mary Shelley's *Frankenstein* revisioned via gleaming machines instead of body parts. A piece of futuristic, extrapolated technology is most often the technological novum that distinguishes a story as SF in the first place, and is, therefore, more than merely a decorative addition to its narrative. More than this, it is the metaphorical effectiveness of technology in SF that focuses the SF encounter with alterity in its most suggestive locus. This is to say that a piece of SF technology – a ray-gun, a spaceship, a time-machine, a matter-transporter – provides a direct, material embodiment of alterity; and that it is exactly because our lives are already surrounded by so many instances of near-miraculous technology, by CD walkmans, by computers, by TV, or by mobile phones, that this novum speaks so directly to us. Technology is something with which we are simultaneously familiar and already estranged from; familiar because it plays so large a part in our life, estranged from because we don't really know how it works, or what the boffins are about to invent next. What this means is that technology focuses our attitude to difference, and that because of this it is often the items of technology that have the most metaphorical potency in an SF text. In this chapter I will look at three key technologies that appear and reappear in SF: the spaceships, the robots and cyberspace. In the first two cases I will look at a number of instances, and explore the ways this hardware functions metaphorically in the SF network of signification. I read the third case with a detailed account of the novel that most famously embodies it, William Gibson's *Neuromancer* (1984).

Isolating the technological features from SF highlights the fact that in most cases technology works in science fiction either directly or obliquely to collapse together the machine and the organic. The bulk of SF technology articulates the trope of the Cyborg, the machine/organic hybrid that is both a special instance of technology and the emblem for all of it. Readers of SF are organic, and the point of relevance of SF technology is that place where the machine intersects the body. Scott Bukatman argues that '*the body*' has long been the repressed content of science fiction, as the genre obsessively substitutes the rational for the corporeal, and the technological for the organic'. As Bukatman points out, nothing repressed stays repressed for very long, and SF texts have 'stage[d] the return of the repressed' by 'construct[ing] their own emphatic, techno-organic reconstructions of the flesh' (Bukatman 1993: 19). The ubiquitous technological trappings of SF, in other words, actually include within them the eruption of the body, of bodies like yours or mine, into the otherwise alienating discourse of the machine.

The key machines of SF are spaceships and robots/computers. The spaceship is almost always humanised: it may be sentient itself, like the frolicsome machines of Iain M Banks's Culture novels, from *Consider Phlebas* (1987) through to *Excession* (1997), or created by joining human and machine, as in Anne McCaffrey's *The Ship Who Sang* (1969), or controlled by a thinking machine like HAL in Arthur C Clarke's *2001: A Space Odyssey*, or, at the very least, imbued with a certain character and individuality like *Star Wars'* *Millennium Falcon*. The spaceship is one focus for the bringing together of human and machine. Robots, more obviously, share human and machine characteristics. Lieutenant Commander Data, from *Star Trek: the Next Generation* aspires to humanity; Superman is organic, but has the strength and endurance of a machine, the 'man of iron'.

In all these cases, what the SF text does is dramatise and characterise our understanding of the alterity of machines. Machines, as the science fiction of Philip K Dick presciently dramatises, can acquire an alarming life of their own. Indeed, in Dick's novels the conventions of SF, with automation, robots – or 'androids', as he calls them, to foreground the human element, *andros* being the Greek for man – and technology, are deployed in a uniquely paranoid manner. As Dick has argued:

> The ultimate in paranoia is not when everyone is against you but when every*thing* is against you. Instead of 'my boss is plotting against me', it would be 'my boss's *phone* is plotting against me.' Objects sometimes seem to possess a will of their own anyhow, to the normal mind; they don't do what

they're supposed to do, they get in the way, they show an unnatural resistance to change.

(Dick, quoted in Freedman 1984: 15)

In Dick's 1969 novel *Ubik*, the protagonist, Joe Chip, finds himself battling with objects as if with people – as in the incident in which he is trying to leave his apartment (his 'conapt'):

He...vigorously strode to the apt door, turned the knob and pulled on the release bolt.

The door refused to open. It said, 'Five cents please.'

He searched his pockets. No more coins; nothing. 'I'll pay you tomorrow,' he told the door. Again he tried the knob. Again it remained locked tight. 'What I pay you,' he informed it, 'is in the nature of a gratuity; I don't *have* to pay you.'

'I think otherwise,' the door said. 'Look in the purchase contract you signed when you bought this conapt.'

In his desk drawer he found the contract; since signing it he had found it necessary to refer to the document many times. Sure enough; payment to his door for opening and shutting constituted a mandatory fee. Not a tip.

'You discover I'm right,' the door said. It sounded smug.

From the drawer beside the sink Joe Chip got a stainless steel knife; with it he began systematically to unscrew the bolt assembly of his apt's money-gulping door.

'I'll sue you,' the door said, as the first screw fell out.

Joe Chip said, 'I've never been sued by a door. But I guess I can live with it.'

(Dick, *Ubik* (1988): 25)

The obvious connection here is a Marxist one; dialectical materialism has focused our attention on the power commodities assume over us ever since *Das Kapital*. Here, for instance, is Marx on tables:

> The form of wood, for instance, is altered if a table is made out of it. Nevertheless the table continues to be wood, an ordinary, sensuous thing. But as soon as it emerges as a commodity it changes into a thing which transcends sensuousness. It not only stands with its feet on the ground but with relation to all other commodities, it stands on its head, and evolves out of its wooden brain grotesque ideas, far more wonderful than if it were to begin dancing of its own free will.
>
> (Marx 1976: 163)

Marx doesn't, of course, mean that tables under capitalism literally start dancing around. But he is pointing up how much power and vitality *things* have when they become part of the exchange of commodities: how people start desiring them, and how they therefore acquire a power over people. In conjunction with the quotation from *Ubik*, this is a suggestive idea. Marx is talking about 'commodity fetishism', what other Marxist thinkers have called 'reification', a word that means literally 'thingification': this raising of 'things' to the status of living objects, this granting to commodities power over us. According to Marx, capitalism is defined as generalised commodity production, which necessarily involves generalised commodity fetishisation. Now, Philip K Dick was certainly not a Marxist in the accepted sense of the term. But his fiction does, again and again, detail the interaction of humanity and fetishised commodities. In his story 'The Days of Perky Pat' (1963), post-nuclear-war communities sit in underground bunkers, their whole lives reduced to games involving 'Barbie and Ken'-style dolls. In 'Captive Market' (1954) and his later novel *The Zap Gun* (1967), even the worldwide arms race resolves into the marketing and production of consumer goods. In *Ubik* (1969), as we have seen, not only doors but all the ordinary adjuncts of Joe Chip's life – his shower, bathroom, fridge, and even his coffee pot – actually underline their role in the exchange-value system by verbally, and none-too-politely, demanding money before each act of use. And in his novel *Do Androids Dream of Electric Sheep?* (1972), human interaction with commodities reaches the ultimate, when the protagonist Rick Deckard actually goes to bed with one, the beautiful android Rachel. The novel is full of 'things': the electric sheep Deckard keeps on his roof, the mood organ he uses to dial up his moods, the 'Mercer' device through which Deckard experiences his religion, and many more. Science fiction as a whole shares much of Dick's dual fascination with and suspicion of the power of things, things that in this mode of writing almost acquire a life of their own.

SPACESHIPS

In the first instance, a spaceship is simply a prop for moving characters around the SF universe; a car or a sailing ship translated into a futuristic idiom. Some spaceships in SF are nothing more than this; George Lucas's X-Wing fighters are figured in the battle scenes of *Star Trek*, as I have argued, as WWII fighter planes relocated to outer space. At the same time, at a more suburban level of cultural symbolism, these spaceships are higher-tech versions of the automobile, the same vehicle that figures so potently in Lucas's earlier movie, *American Graffiti* (1973). That film is a cinematic reworking of Lucas's own small-town adolescence; and, in a more obviously coded way, so are the *Star Wars* films. Luke Skywalker (Luke S., a cipher for Lucas) can climb into his X-Wing fighter and 'drive' across the galaxy, to park outside Yoda's jungle home, before 'driving' back to join his friends for the finale. It would not be correct to say that these sorts of spaceship are 'just' facilitators, because they are themselves fetishised, something that is evidenced by the fascination of fans with collecting models or getting hold of pseudo-technical specifications for these machines. But they do exist on a level where the metaphorical sense has not yet spilled over into Ship-as-Cyborg.

I should elaborate what I mean by this, because it is important to the argument I am making. Spaceships in SF come in two sorts; those that are 'just' machines, like cars, and those that are more than just machines, that can think for themselves, express personality and character, or that represent a combination of the human and the technological, such as McCaffrey's *Ship That Sang*. The *Millennium Falcon*, to take another example from *Star Wars*, is one of the former sort. It has more individuality than an X-Wing fighter, perhaps even a degree of 'personality' of its own, a cussed, ornery sort of personality, but this is only true in the way in which your old car may develop crotchets and quirks. It is a different sort of thing from *The Liberator*, the spaceship from the British TV series *Blake's-7*, which possessed a computer mind of its own called 'Zen'. And yet, in one important respect, the *Millennium Falcon* is more than the sum of its parts. This is because the spaceships in an SF film are invested by us with a peculiar, almost human concentration of value: Marxist 'reification'. In a postmodern culture such as our own, the power and autonomy of commodities reach almost the level where Philip K Dick's 'Joe Chip' dilemma becomes our own.

In the context of SF, this reification works most potently on the interconnected levels of representation of technology and the technologies of reproduction. Putting the matter crudely, people queuing up to see the latest *Star Wars* film are in large part waiting precisely to see the special effects. It is those effects which are so 'cool', which can dwarf the appeals of things like 'character' and 'plot'. It is possible to imagine a film where the plot and characterisation are utterly risible, but where the special effects are cool enough to mean that SF fans still take it to their hearts. Indeed, we really don't need to imagine this; we can think of many actual examples. Critics, and particularly film reviewers, sometimes complain about the dominance of special effects, but that is missing the point. The special effects in any given SF film – and, in a slightly different way, the technical marvels of more conventional written SF – *are* the point. The X-Wing fighters hurtling into the teeth of another space battle are characters in a very real sense. This is what reification means, and in critical terms one key effect is that, even when they are 'merely' hardware, or 'merely' facilitators, spaceships are still, in effect, cyborgs. They are both technology, like the blasters, *and* characters, like Han Solo or C3PO. This is why fans go to specialist shops and buy models of Tie-Fighters.

The richness of the situation, critically speaking, is that this reification of technology in SF cinema is actually a *self-reflexive* factor. The technology we fans admire so completely, the spaceships that we consider so cool and which are deployed on the screen before us in so exciting a fashion, are nothing more than the external trapping of the technology that we are *really* admiring, the technology of cinema itself. To say this is to connect with the theories of the postmodernist thinker Jean Baudrillard, who argues that the media imitation of 'reality' which he calls the 'simulacrum' has so replaced the real that it is all we have left. 'Reality' has been replaced by the *hyperreality* of our simulated world. In the realm of the Baudrillardian simulacrum, it is the technologies of simulation themselves that rule. This might appear to be a rather far-fetched claim, but it merits further consideration. Science as simulation is the reason why fictional science, or 'SF', is so much more exciting than *real* science; why *Star Wars* is more fun to watch than a real shuttle launch; why the adventures of the real-life space shuttle *Enterprise* were so much less enthralling than the adventures of the fictional USS *Enterprise*. The technologies of reproduction, particularly in the realm of special effects, are at a far more advanced stage of development than the actual technologies of space exploration. This also explains, I think, the contradictions experienced by those watching something like the *Challenger* disaster, in which a manned space shuttle exploded on ascent. On the one hand, this was something clearly appalling and tragic, something that moved many people to tears as it happened. But on another level, the live TV pictures bumped people from one mode of watching to another, and gave a guilty undertow to the emotions. The *Challenger* launch was certainly the most memorable and, in a terrible way, the most exciting of all the shuttle launches; and shuttle launches are renowned for being dull, for always being delayed and postponed, and then for providing just another version of all the other shuttle launches we have seen when they finally happen. What *Challenger* did was suddenly to shift modes: from the 'real' mode of an actual launch to the 'SFX' mode of a film. In SF films spaceships explode all the time, and it is exciting. When *Challenger* exploded, the moment collapsed together our perceptions; that was one reason why, apart from being so terrible, it was so unsettling.

What spaceships do, then, in cinematic SF is focus our fascination with the medium itself. Spaceships are symbolic nova, but self-reflexive ones; and this is true of most SF hardware in one shape or another. To stay with *Star Wars* for a moment, there are two sorts of spaceships in these films: the very big, and the ordinary-sized, which is to say, the car- or truck-sized. The very big – the Imperial Cruisers, for instance, or the Death Star – are about technological *scale*; in effect, they are saying 'the technologies of cinema present us with very big things: sublime enormities on a screen much, much bigger than a TV screen'. The ordinary-sized are about issues of technological *speed*: X-Wings zooming along a trench in the side of the Death Star; the rapidity with which the technologies of cinema move things along; the excitements of speeding us through a narrative; and at root a fetishisation of the increasing speed of Western culture. Spaceships are the emblems of the technology that produces them; a technology of cultural reproduction, rather than science.

This seems clear enough in cinematic terms, but it is also the case in a great deal of written SF too. Iain M Banks's 'Culture' novels include as characters both organic humanoids and sentient spaceships; indeed, it is the ships who are generally the more interesting characters. By interesting, I mean the more quirkily humorous, the more engaged, the more intelligent. Banks's characters have cod-genre names, heavy on the consonants: 'Rasd-Coduresa Diziet', 'Ky', 'Rogtam-Bar' and the like. But his spaceships have names like 'Very Little Gravitas Indeed', 'What Are The Civilian Applications?' and 'Congenital Optimist', and senses of humour to match. When, in *Use of Weapons* (1990), the organic protagonist is injured so severely that only his head remains, and has to be regrown in a sort of cloning vat, he himself provides us with a series of agonised reflections of mutilation and pain. It is his robotic companion who gives us the more comical perspective by buying him a hat. The point here is that it is exactly for the witty, cynical and urbane tone of Banks's writing that people love his books so much; and that that tone is emblematised predominantly in the machine, rather than the humanoid, characterisation.

Another way of working this metaphorical representation is through capaciousness, in other words through sheer size and scale. With works such as C J Cherryh's 'Merchanters' series (beginning with the popular *Downbelow Station* in 1981), spaceships are more than facilitators; they are where people live. There is a branch of SF that insists on working within the constraints of Einsteinian physics, such that trips between stars have to take place at speeds less than that of light, and therefore take decades or even centuries. In many examples of this SF the characters are compelled to live on their spaceships as worlds. The metaphor here seems straightforward enough: the spaceship is the world. In fact, as I have been arguing, the spaceship is actually 'the world of the text', which is to say, 'the world of SF'. The spaceship in Brian Aldiss's *NonStop* (1958) is revealed to be a spaceship rather than a self-contained world only towards the end of the text: in other words, until the end we take the technological artefact to *be* organic.

Another famous spaceship, the *Discovery* from *2001: A Space*

Odyssey, is part inanimate hardware, part thinking machine (the computer HAL). The disjunction between these two elements is emphasised by the voice of HAL, a softly spoken, breathy and warm voice that gains its sinister power in large part through how 'organic' it sounds, in stark contrast with both the inhumanly clean, antiseptic environment provided inside the ship and the scaffolding-and-sphere shape of the ship from the outside. When the computer goes mad, it does two things. On one level it crosses over from the conceptual territory of 'the machine' to that of the human: which is to say, where before it could play chess, or engage in conversation, things we all accept that both humans and computers can do, after it does something we associate primarily with human beings: it becomes paranoid, kills, begs for its life and so on. But, on a different level, it gives us the sense that it is only making explicit something we have always half-wondered, half-feared of machines. It is the Joe Chip moment again, the paranoid sense that machines all possess the potential to turn on us, to go mad, to express their character.

The *Star Trek* films, taken as a sequence, are fascinated by a particular narrative pattern of death and resurrection, but the interesting thing is that they make little distinction between a specific organic and a technological death/rebirth. *Star Trek 2: the Wrath of Khan* (1982) ends climactically with the death of Spock, who sacrifices himself to give the others a chance for life. *Star Trek 3: the Search for Spock* (1984) is structured similarly: it concerns the coming-back-to-life of Spock, but also includes at a climactic moment the death of the starship *Enterprise*, destroyed by Kirk to give the crew a chance for life. Kirk's grief in both texts is equally heartfelt. 'What have I done?' he asks in *Star Trek 3*, horrified with himself. 'What you had to do,' replies his friend, McCoy. 'Turned death into a fighting chance for life.' And, following the logic of the film, the *Enterprise* is reborn at the end of *Star Trek 4: the Voyage Home* (1986) in much the same way that Spock had been at the end of *Star Trek 3*. The characters of Spock, and 'the *Enterprise*' are well chosen here: not only is Spock the most machine-like character in *Star Trek*, the most rational and coldly logical, but the *Enterprise* is amongst the most humanised examples of spaceship technology.

Paul McAuley's 'Confluence' novels, *Child of the River* (1997), *Ancients of Days* (1998) and *Shrine of Stars* (1999), take this to a logical extreme. Confluence is an enormous world built long ago by human beings who raised up to sentience an enormous range of animals from all around the galaxy to inhabit it. It is a flat world with an artificial gravity operating across its surface that rocks back and forth to mimic sunrise and sunset. The makers of this enormous artefact, known as the Preservers, have long since fled the universe through a nearby black hole, but their creations continue to worship them as gods. The world of Confluence is one in which both machines and organic life interact in the fullest way imaginable. Billions of machines, from the enormous engines in the keel of the world to the myriad insect-like tiny machines that fly hither and thither through the sky, work constantly to maintain the world. The organic component of Confluence is similarly diverse, with a systematically encyclopaedic range of animals given quasi-human consciousness and a range of approximations to human shape. Yama, the hero, is a point of connection: he is the only remaining example of the bloodline of the Builders, and as such he has telepathic control over the machines. He functions, in other words, as the point of connection between organic and technological. At the trilogy's conclusion, Confluence itself disintegrates and reveals itself to be a conglomeration of innumerable giant spaceships, 'the great ships which the Builders had joined together in the first act of the creation of the world' (McAuley, *Shrine of Stars* (1999): 312). These ships eventually fall apart again, 'a cloud of splinters shining in the light of the lonely star', on voyages to reoccupy the abandoned galaxy. Confluence becomes the seed from which organic life can grow throughout the cosmos.

ROBOTS

We get the word 'robot' from Czech author Karel Capek's play
R.U.R. (1921), where the word is used to refer to automatic
labourers of organic origin, what today we would be more likely
to call 'androids'. Through the 1920s and 1930s there were a
large number of robot stories published, either representing the
men-machines as Frankenstein's-Monster-style threats, or else
using them to explore the boundaries between human and
machine. Perhaps the most famous robot storywriter was Isaac
Asimov, who generally wrote the latter sort of story. With John
Campbell, editor of *Astounding*, he formulated the 'three laws of
robotics', which all robots in his imaginative universe must follow:

(1) a robot may not injure a human being or, through inaction,
allow a human being to come to harm;

(2) a robot must obey the orders given it by human beings
except where such orders would conflict with the First Law;

(3) a robot must protect its own existence as long as such pro-
tection does not conflict with the First or Second Law.

Asimov's 'robot' stories revolve largely around the narrative
potentials inherent in exploring or contravening these rules; and,
as with many of the definitions of SF we have looked at so far,
there's something self-defeating in this sort of precision. We
think of Paul Verhoeven's witty if violent *Robocop* (1987), where
the central cyborg policeman/robot is constrained by a similarly
binding but more international capitalist set of rules. When the
villain, a corporation employee, takes the corporation president
hostage, Robocop can do nothing, because he is programmed not
to harm any corporation members; but when the president,
understandably furious, yells 'you're fired!' at the villain holding
him prisoner, Robocop is freed from restraints and can shoot him

dead. The effect, in the film, is comic; but the *point* presumably has to do with the arbitrariness and fragility of the rules that prevent machines from turning on us. The form of alterity represented by machines – the uncanny irruption of the inhuman into the sphere of the human – is both comical *and* sinister.

Asimov's 'robot' stories have a different emphasis. The main effect of his 'three laws of robotics' is to foreground the *ethical* in the delineation of the machine. Asimov's robots are supremely ethical machines, governed in the first instance by a desire to preserve and aid human life. Because the ethical imperative is so central to their conception, Asimov's robots are necessarily attractive and humanised creations. In terms of the representation of difference, they embody a mapping onto a technological framework of more everyday social differences. As Edward James puts it, 'it is difficult not to see Asimov's *Caves of Steel* (1953), with its robots who take ordinary people's jobs and even "pass for human", as a comment upon relations between whites and blacks in America' (James 1994: 89).

The sinister potential of 'the robot' has provided many SF texts with their organising structure. In Michael Crichton's *Westworld* (1973), fun-seekers can spend a holiday in a recreation of the wild west, or of medieval England or ancient Rome, peopled by robots. In Westworld itself, holidaymakers are given guns with sensors that distinguish human from machine, so they can shoot the robots to their heart's content but can't accidentally injure one another. Things, of course, go wrong, something signified by the fact that the robot gunslinger Yul Brynner starts killing people. Apparently the guns, and the robots themselves, no longer distinguish human from machine. A cameo at the end of the film emphasises this: the protagonist, having escaped death at the hands of the malfunctioning gunslinger robot, finds a woman chained in a dungeon begging for water. He gives her a drink and thereby fuses her circuits: she had been a robot all along. It is impossible to tell human and machine apart.

In Ridley Scott's *Alien* (1979), crewmember Ash, played by Ian Holm, is an android with sinister intentions that include murdering his crewmates if necessary. But the confusion between human and machine goes beyond the fact that his crewmates, and the audience, don't realise that he is a machine until late in the film. More than this is the fact that, unlike the 'dry' technology of electrical circuitry that lies beneath Yul Brynner's artificial skin in *Westworld*, Ash is constructed out of an organic-looking 'wet' technology, so that when injured he spurts out what we take to be hydraulic fluid, and his viscera are a series of disconcerting slippery tubes and conduits. In Bukatman's words, 'the android, Ash, is both organic and inorganic as well, and "his" destruction is marked by the gushing forth of the milky fluids that constitute "his" "blood"' (Bukatman 1993: 266). There is something inherently unsettling about this superimposition of organic and machine, something that finds its most efficient expression in the robot for the obvious reason that robots are designed precisely to look like human beings. Ridley Scott's cinematic version of Dick's *Do Androids Dream of Electric Sheep?*, the film *Blade Runner* (1982), presents its robots, or 'replicants', as fleshly machines that breathe, bleed and eventually die precisely in order to be able to work through questions relating to how we define 'human'. Scott's replicants look human, and are in fact represented as childlike. Designed with only four years of life, they have – despite their adult bodies and intelligence – many of the unformed attitudes of children. This is in spite of the fact that they are ruthless killers who murder a number of people in the course of the film. When the chief replicant, Roy, steps into the apartment of the human Sebastian, which is full of life-size mechanised automata, he speaks like an excited child: 'Gosh – you've got a lot of great toys here!' Confronting the fact that all their fellow replicants have died, the female robot Pris responds, not with grief, but instead with a petulant line delivered with the intonation of a two-year-old: 'but then we're stupid and we'll die!' It is this combination of human, childlike innocence and ingenuousness, with a machine-like strength and ruthlessness, that provides the replicants with their uncanny metaphoric potency.

In other words, the robot is that place in an SF text where technological and human are most directly blended. The robot is the dramatisation of the alterity of the machine, the paranoid sense of the inorganic come to life. That it works this way, rather than just clothing the human in mechanical dress, is indicated by a few key examples. When Douglas Adams fictionalises a robot with what his 'Sirius Cybernetics Corporation' calls 'Genuine People Personalities' or 'GPPs', the result can only be expressed in a comic mode. Adams's *Hitchhiker's Guide to the Galaxy*, a radio series from the late 1970s and early 1980s, is a deft and often hilarious satire on many SF tropes. But it is Marvin, the enormously intelligent but chronically depressed android, whose metallic clanking and the hydraulic puffs and gasps accompanying his movement suggest that he is more robot than android, who remains one of the most enduring creations of the series. Marvin combines the attributes of the most advanced of machine intelligences with the pathological character traits of a particularly flawed human being. He has, as he repeatedly insists, 'a brain the size of a planet'; he is so intelligent that he can read human consciousness; and he is so durable that he can, and in one episode does, live from now until the literal end of the universe, however many billennia that represents. 'You mean you can see into my mind?' asks the incredulous human character, Arthur Dent. 'And?' 'It amazes me,' says Marvin, gloomily, 'how you manage to live in anything so small.' But at the same time he is so continually depressed and miserable that it is a chore having to be around him; he hates everything, including himself, and he is able literally to bore some security guards to death merely by telling them his miserable life story. The joke, that robots given 'Genuine People Personalities' might also develop Genuine People Personality Disorders, might seem a thin one to spin out over twelve episodes, but the glory of Marvin's characterisation is that he pursues the expression of his depression with machine-like rigour, so that he not only adds human characteristics to his machineness, he adds machine characteristics to his human traits. He is a potently thorough blending of machine and man.

By now the terms of the debate have shifted from technology as such, and onto that creature I touched on first in Chapter 3 and again earlier in the present chapter: the Cyborg. We have already encountered Donna Harraway's influential essay on the cyborg, a quasi-feminist manifesto aimed at reclaiming the positive aspects of cyborg existence. But Harraway is quite forthright about the 'perversity' of her positive feminist re-appropriation of this SF icon. The reason for this is that, Marvin aside, most SF cyborgs have used their unsettling connotations to represent evil. A figure such as Arnold Schwarzenegger's embodiment of a killer cyborg sets himself absolutely against humanity. As Jonathan Goldberg points out, 'The Terminator embodies a "new order of intelligence" that is resolutely anti-human and anti-reproductive.' His task in the movie 'is nothing less than a mission to ensure the end of the human race' (Gray *et al.* 1995: 243). Even here, though, the representation of difference in the shape of the cyborg has its interesting potentials. One populist manifestation of the cyborg, the Borg from the *Star Trek* franchises, actually forces the issue of alterity in a radical manner, taking the revaluation of all values to its logical extreme. Bringing together organic and machine in a stylishly designed package, the Borg represent the most extreme foe the Federation has yet encountered. The Borg appeared in certain *Next Generation* episodes, most notably 'The Best of Both Worlds', and were so popular with fans that they have been often resurrected. It is interesting to consider exactly what is so appealing to *Trek* fans about the Borg.

One of the points of audience connection with the Borg, it seems to me, is precisely their old-fashionedness. Their technology, although being, as many characters repeatedly assert, greatly superior to anything the Federation has, *looks* very old. The styling of the Borg is retrograde; all those tubes and whirring devices, and the tiny little revolving satellite dishes on the top of their heads, are old-fashioned, like something out of the 1950s: you won't find any satellite dishes whirring on the sleekly futuristic *Enterprise*. Moreover, because they are 'old-fashioned', the Borg enact the fertile contradiction at the heart of SF, the collision of future and past, of prophetic and nostalgic modes. There is another way in which we, as audience, register this retro difference: the Borg are 'black and white', not just in the sense that their costumes are black leather and plastic and their skin pale, but in a more literal sense. In 'The Best of Both Worlds', Captain Picard is captured by the Borg and turned into a drone; in one scene the Captain is on a Borg operating table, and a probe of some kind is inserted into the side of his head, causing the colour literally to drain from his face. It is as if the Borg belong to a realm of black-and-white film; and this contrast is emphasised by the first team to beam over to the Borg ship from the *Enterprise*: the colourful uniforms of the members of this team (actually primary colours: Shelby in Red, Crusher in Blue, Worf and Data in Yellow) seem garish in the colour-restricted environment of the Borg ship. We might argue that the Borg point to a cinematic aesthetic; that they are emblematic representatives of clunky black-and-white cinema, whilst the *Enterprise* belongs in the world of colour TV.

The Borg 'collective', in which all individuality is utterly squashed and everyone works for the good of the whole, appears at first sight as a rather crude satire on communism, pitted against the 'American' individuality of the *Enterprise* crew. But the Borg have a vitality (paradoxically) that supersedes any one narrowly allegorical reading of their significance. Taylor Harrison, for example, sees the Borg as representative of death, or, more specifically, he has read the Borg episodes of *Next Generation* as a coded representation of the AIDS epidemic (Harrison 1996: 257).

The *Next Generation* film *First Contact*, as another example, sees the Borg reimagined not as communists but as vampires. And more potently, I think, is the way 'The Best of Both Worlds' expresses one aspect of the vigorous American zeitgeist, alien abduction. Communism, and the evil Russian Empire, is old news, the dustbin of history. Alien abduction, on the other hand, is bang up-to-date, one of the key narratives of contemporary USA. The scenes where Picard, who has been, quite literally, abducted by aliens, is laid out on some sort of operating table and has probes inserted into his head is the most explicit reference to this cultural narrative. But over and above these partial interpretations of the Borg is the fact that they remain one of the most thorough, most effective attempts by SF writers working in a popular idiom to represent an alterity that is genuinely other.

The emphasis upon alterity expands our sense of the radical otherness of the Borg in this context. The Borg as they originally appear represent everything the Federation is not, focusing our attention on the way their mode of being is literally beyond our ability to comprehend. This is the true nature of 'otherness'; that an alien would be not 'basically like you or me but with pointy ears' (like Spock), but instead radically and totally unlike you or me or anything we can conceive. So, where Federation, which is to say human, culture is based on individuality, on what Picard proudly insists in the face of the Borg ship is 'freedom and self-determination', the Borg culture is not. Where human culture is hierarchical, so that Picard is in charge, with everybody else on the *Enterprise* ranked in some set position beneath him, there are no ranks or hierarchies on the Borg ship. The Federation is a *centred* civilisation; which is to say, it is literally centred on what the series refers to several times as 'sector zero zero one', or Earth; and also metaphorically centred on certain core values, the beliefs and ideologies at the centre of human existence which give purpose and meaning to our lives. The Borg have no centre; they have no purpose or meaning, and don't need them. The postmodern theory of contemporary French thinkers Gilles Deleuze and Felix Guattari distinguishes between on the one hand the 'arboreal' or 'tree-like' logics of more traditional cultures, which like a tree function in one up–down direction, are hierarchical and restricted; and on the other hand the 'rhizomatic' or 'root-like' logics of postmodernism – which, like a system of roots under the soil, make all manner of interesting connections in all sorts of directions and dimensions. According to this postmodern perspective, the Borg are rhizomatic, decentred and associative; the Federation, on the other hand, is arboreal, centred and structured. The Borg do without notions of 'individuality', of 'centre' or 'structure', of 'purpose' or 'meaning'; they have, as Worf gruffly points out, 'neither Honor nor Courage' and have no need of them. They do not value any of the things that we value: they dismiss, in turn, 'strength', 'freedom', 'self-determination' and 'death'. In fact, they seem to do without the very notion of 'value'. This, I suggest, is a bold stab by the *Star Trek* scriptwriters at presenting something *radically* other, something with which the human-centred Federation really has nothing in common. To emphasise the point, the boldness here is in *doing the representing*. There are SF texts, such as *2001* or *Contact*, which are prepared to posit a radical otherness in their aliens, but they also duck out of the challenge of representing it. Not so *Star Trek*. It is this sense of utter difference, of a discontinuity which cannot be breached, that underlies what have always struck me as some of the most chillingly effective lines in TV science fiction. When the captured Picard is taken aboard the Borg ship and argues with the disembodied voice of the Borg, he seems, literally, to be speaking to the whole ship. Picard states the key values of the Federation, the key values, arguably, of any 'life form', and in each case the Borg simply negate them, ultimately negating life itself. They do this not in the sense that they 'value' destroying life or killing, as a warrior race might, but rather in the utterly other sense that neither life nor death is of any importance.

PICARD: I will resist you with my last ounce of strength.

THE BORG: Strength is irrelevant. Resistance is futile...Your culture will adapt to service ours.

PICARD: Impossible! My culture is based on freedom and self-determination.

THE BORG: Freedom is irrelevant. Self-determination is irrelevant. You must comply.

PICARD: We would rather die.

THE BORG: Death is irrelevant.

The power of this exchange resides less in the way the Borg assert something, for instance that they are 'stronger' than the Federation and can force complicity: after all, as they say, 'strength is irrelevant'. More powerful is their extraordinary statement of values, or rather of anti-values. The construction that such-and-such 'is irrelevant' does not even engage in a dialectic with the thing in question, because to do that would be to suggest that because the Borg are prepared to engage with it the thing in question has some value. But they are utterly dismissive. The Borg do not say 'your strength is insufficient', which, by implication, would imply 'we value our superior strength'. Instead they say 'strength', with the implication of all strength, yours, ours, 'is irrelevant'. It does not figure. Similarly, and most radically, they do not even value life, the being that is most basic to any humanist conception of existence. It is impossible for us to enter imaginatively into the world of the Borg because certain key values we hold, values like individuality, life/death and so on, are too centrally part of us, whereas for the Borg they are neither good nor bad but simply irrelevant. This is why it is hard to avoid the conclusion that the subsequent Borg episodes of *Star Trek*, and especially the film, constitute an enormous let-down.

After striving to contemplate a genuine alienness, an otherness outwith our capacities to conceive, the remaining Borg episodes fall away. The point of 'I, Borg', a later episode of *The Next Generation* in which Geordi brings forth the individuality of an isolated Borg, seems a sort of betrayal of the original conception. It is as if once having established that, for the Borg, individuality is irrelevant, the makers of *Next Generation* have recoiled, retreated, have said to themselves, 'Well, yes, alright, but surely individuality cannot be completely *irrelevant* to the Borg. After all, individuality matters so very much to me, it cannot be simply absent in Borg culture, so it must just be suppressed. In "I, Borg" we will show that buried individuality being unearthed.' But the result of this is to rob the Borg of their distinctiveness, their alienness: they are no longer, it seems, a culture for which individuality is irrelevant; they are a culture where individuality is suppressed, which makes their culture like an Earth tyranny. The greatest betrayal of the conception of the Borg as other, though, comes in the film *First Contact*, which goes against the entire point of the Borg. In 'The Best of Both Worlds' the Borg are a genuinely rhizomatic and decentred species, something quite new to *Star Trek*, and to most SF. But *First Contact* implausibly reveals that the Borg are not decentred; that, on the contrary, they are highly centred. They have a Queen, and that Queen can relate to Picard and Data in exactly the way any other *Star Trek* alien, or any human, might do. This involves an unavoidable sense of the belittlement of the conception of the Borg as radically other.

CYBERSPACE

'Cyberspace' is a term in increasing currency today. It refers to the notional space of the internet and virtual reality, to the computer-generated environments into which human beings can enter through a computer or a virtual-reality suit. In reality this 'space' is fairly limited, but many science-fiction texts posit a time when cyberspace is an exciting and dynamic realm of possibilities. Its cognate SF sub-genre is Cyberpunk.

Cyberpunk is that contemporary mode of SF most implicated with technology. Indeed, Samuel Delany sees all cyberpunk as necessarily pro-technology, as a way of seeing and representing the world that prioritises the technological over the psychological, with obvious implications for the kind of fiction written under its aegis.

> Cyberpunk is pro-tech, it is apsychological...Cyberspace exists merely as a technological consensus. Without that technology it could not exist, be entered, or function. It's much closer to Popper's notion of 'World-3' (the world of texts and data that interweaves and stabilizes the world of human beings) or Chardin's 'Noosphere' (the circle of abstract knowledges presumed to be generated by and encircling the biosphere) than it is to anything internal or psychological.
>
> (Delany 1994: 176)

George Slusser says something similar when he classifies SF as 'an infosphere', with cyberpunk as the 'informational conscience' of genre.

> In the cyberpunk world, to write SF is to make physical, even visceral contact with the mechanical and biological extensions of our personal infosphere (cyborgs, grafts, prostheses, clones), and beyond that with the image surrogates themselves (simulations, 'constructs', holograms) that now crowd and share our traditional fictional living space.
>
> (Slusser and Shippey 1992: 3)

Slusser's point has something to do with the materiality of SF, which I discussed earlier; the way SF provides concrete, material externalisations for metaphors of alterity. But he is also suggesting a close enough affinity between SF as literature and the reality of existence in the West today under the cultural logic critics call 'postmodernism'. We encountered this earlier, in Baudrillard's argument that contemporary culture involves us in a supersession of reality by simulacra. The extent to which postmodernism as a cultural logic depends upon today's advanced technology is rarely stressed by critics of that phenomenon; but it is precisely that technology – and most especially today's technologies of mass reproduction: the TV, the computer – that determines and defines postmodernity. And it is the coming together of TV and computer that informs cyberspace, one of the most potent of the technological metaphors to come out of SF.

CASE STUDY: WILLIAM GIBSON, *NEUROMANCER* (1984)

Cyberspace as a term and a concept seems to have been invented by Bruce Sterling, but to have gained wide currency with the publication of William Gibson's *Neuromancer* (1984). Actually, far from being a celebration of technology, Gibson's novel articulates a distinctively double-edged attitude to the machine. On the one hand, this is a text that delights in the ingenious and fascinating toys its imaginative universe produces; although given the spy/crime genre Gibson is working in, this delight is expressed chiefly in terms of the damage the technology can do: how effective the weaponry is, how deadly Molly's implants are, and so on. But simultaneously the technology in this imaginative universe is almost always threatening, alienating, a negative quantity. The fact that his technology is always what antique dealers call 'distressed', that is to say the creation of a sense of rough edges, broken components and all-round decay, is one of the most noteworthy features of the Gibsonian style. In part his novel reads like an aesthetic attack on the notion of technology itself, a sort of textual bashing of the stuff of the narrative. One of the things Gibson does best is create the same sense of ambient technological paranoia that Philip K Dick achieves so perfectly, and Dick's *Ubik* serves as a sort of intertextual template here. The Gibsonian universe presents a world where humans battle to survive in an urban jungle; but the most dangerous predators in this jungle are the machines. At times Gibson eerily captures exactly the unease with which we can regard the familiar technological props of our own lives, such as phones, TVs and microwaves – the way in which they seem almost to have a life of their own. His character Case's first encounter with Wintermute, the Artificial Intelligence or 'AI' that is arguably the novel's chief protagonist, manages this tone of technology-paranoid sensibility perfectly. Case is buying cigarettes from a vending machine next to a line of phones:

> He fumbled through a pocketful of lirasi, slotting the dull alloy coins one after another, vaguely amused by the anachronism of the process. The phone nearest him rang.
>
> Automatically, he picked it up.
>
> 'Yeah?'
>
> Faint harmonics, tiny inaudible voices rattling across some orbital link, and then a sound like wind.
>
> 'Hello, Case.'
>
> A fifty-lirasi coin fell from his hand, bounced, and rolled out of sight across Hilton carpeting.
>
> 'Wintermute, Case. It's time we talk.'
>
> It was a chip voice.
>
> 'Don't you want to talk, Case?'
>
> He hung up.
>
> On his way back to the lobby, his cigarettes forgotten, he had to walk the length of the ranked phones. Each rang in turn, but only once, as he passed.
>
> (Gibson, *Neuromancer* (1984): 121)

This is a very nicely balanced piece of writing. Gibson knows when to stress the down-to-earth, to dwell on the quotidian details like the tedium of having to feed coins into a vending machine, a detail made doubly tedious in this context of a future world where such devices are almost obsolete. He also knows how to prepare the ground for the chill, the surprise, by suddenly dropping in a sentence in a more self-consciously 'poetic' idiom, signalled by the lack of main verb as much as the quasi-mystical echoes of the Bible: 'Faint harmonics…and then a sound like wind.' And making the phone the first pseudo-supernatural agent of Wintermute's appearance is appropriate too. Of all our present-day technologies, phones have had a pedigree of spooking people. The very idea of voices whispering to us from the other side of the world is something which partakes of spiritualism and the uncanny.

This notion of haunting is behind the ethical conceit of the novel as well; in so far as the novel explores an ethical grey-area, it has to do with whether Wintermute 'should' or 'shouldn't' be allowed to upgrade itself, to become more perfect and complete, and possibly fully sentient. Wintermute itself sees this as an evolutionary matter: 'You're always building models. Stone circles. Cathedrals. Pipe Organs. Adding machines. I got no idea why I'm here, you know that? But if the run goes off tonight, you'll have finally managed the real thing' (p. 204). Other characters in the novel see it in terms of a pact with the Devil; as Wintermute says, 'The French girl, she said you were selling out the species. Demon, she said I was…it doesn't much matter' (p. 205). The French girl, Michele, conceives the terms of the exchange as a throwback negotiation, this being the first place where the resonances of the 'neuromancer' [necromancer] title start to bite:

> 'You are worse than a fool,' Michele said, getting to her feet, the pistol in her hand. 'You have no care for your species. For thousands of years men dreamed of pacts with demons. Only now are such things possible. And what would you be paid with?'
>
> (Gibson, *Neuromancer* (1984): 193)

This is the atavistic scheme underlying the apparently forward-looking ethos of the novel; and it is at this point that technology and magic become, as is often the case in SF, only a matter of perspective. In this sense, *Neuromancer* is as nostalgic, as backward-looking an American SF text, as any.

Cyberpunk, more thoroughly and systematically than any other SF novum, is built around the process of metaphor. Cyberspace itself is not a real space, but a notional space, a metaphorical space. In Gibson's novel it is described in literal, visual terms, although the narrative repeats several times that it is not a literal or visual space, but rather a 'nonspace' (p. 81). Gibson conceded that this imaginary environment was based, not on any personal experience of the world of computing – since he had no such experience – but upon the video games his children played. Accordingly, description in *Neuromancer* often adopts an almost facile, video-gamelike quality:

> Faint kaleidoscopic angles centred in to a silver-black point. Case watched childhood symbols of evil and bad luck tumble out along translucent planes: swastikas, skulls and cross-bones, dice flashing snake eyes...[At the core there was] a shark thing, gleaming like obsidian...'That's the sting,' the construct said.
>
> (Gibson, *Neuromancer* (1984): 216)

On this level, there is an almost small-minded literalism about Gibson's cyberspace: a programme designed to protect information appears as a shark, scattering signs of ill omen around it. But what this space does is to articulate the action of metaphor: this defensive programme will not only 'bite' you *like* an angry shark, it actually *is* an angry shark, at least in the world it inhabits. The same holds for 'ICE', a substance that gets its name simply enough from its acronym: it is a software that protects against intrusion, and so is called 'Intrusion Countermeasure Electronics'.

But when we encounter 'ICE' in the world of Gibson's cyberspace, it functions at both levels at once, as metaphor and as literalism:

> Ice patterns formed and reformed on the screen as he probed for gaps, skirted the most obvious traps, and mapped the route he'd take through Sense/Net's ice. It was good ice. Wonderful ice. Its patterns burned there while he lay with his arm under Molly's shoulders.
>
> (Gibson, *Neuromancer* (1984): 76)

A great deal of Gibson's prose mediates in this fashion between the literal and the metaphorical; and the overall effect for the novel as a whole is to create a finely balanced textual construct, something that could go either way, capable of being read either as a gritty-realist account of actual existence, or as a symbolist text, almost an allegory, of the epistemological hunt, the search of knowledge and meaning.

This double perspective feeds through into all sorts of aspects of Gibson's descriptive world. Take this description of cyberspace:

> He punched himself through and found an infinite blue space ranged with color-coded spheres strung on a tight grid of pale blue neon. In the nonspace of the matrix, the interior of a given data construct possessed unlimited subjective dimension; a child's toy calculator, accessed through Case's Sendai, would have presented limitless gulfs of nothingness hung with a few basic commands.
>
> (Gibson, *Neuromancer* (1984): 81)

What is oxymoronic about this piece of description at a localised level – which is to say, how can this space be both a 'tight grid' and an 'infinite blue space'; how can 'neon' be 'pale' and so on – actually only figures the larger sense in which Gibson deliberately unsettles our textual expectations in order to convey the paradoxical status of this space. The effect of this, in the end, is almost spiritual – which is one reason why the Japanese figuring of this tale, both the technology used in it and the actual setting for many scenes, is so appropriate. Underlying this streetwise, distressed-tech narrative is an almost Zen artistic vision, where infinity can be glimpsed in the simplest thing, where a 'child's toy calculator' can present 'limitless gulfs of nothingness' to the trained perception. The effect of *this* is presumably to elevate cyberspace into a near-magical realm, a realm where humanity is freed from the constraints of the flesh, what the novel calls 'meat', so that we can soar like the angels. Cyberspace becomes an almost religious experience. Compare, for instance, the way the book's first sex-scene describes orgasm: Case and Molly have sex 'until they both had come, his orgasm flaring blue in timeless space, a vastness like the matrix, where the faces were shredded and blown away down hurricane corridors' (p. 45). It is as if orgasm, briefly, reaches the peak where cyberspace is all the time; that, by implication, cyberspace is the ultimate intensity of physical experience.

This metaphorical theme inhabits all the levels of the text. It is there in the prose style, the building blocks of the novel, and it is also there on the level of the novel's conception, the metaphor that is cyberspace. But it goes deeper than that. Of the characters who appear in the novel, some are 'real' characters, some are 'constructs', or more accurately metaphors standing in for characters. But how easy is it to distinguish between these different sorts of character? Case's erstwhile colleague Dix is an interesting example. Case resurrects this character from death, something articulated in the flat matrix of the novel without Biblical or religious overtones, such that even the tag 'Lazarus of cyberspace' (p. 98) functions as a blank reference. Dix comes back as a 'construct'. To begin with he is 'directionless' in more senses than one:

[Case] coughed. 'Dix? McCoy? That you man?' His throat was tight.

'Hey bro,' said a directionless voice.

'It's Case, man. Remember?'

'Miami, joeboy, quick study.'

'What's the last thing you remember before I spoke to you, Dix?'

'Nothin'.

'Hang on.' He disconnected the construct. The presence was gone.

He reconnected it. 'Dix? Who am I?'

'You got me hung, Jack. Who the fuck are you?'

'Ca – your buddy. Partner. What's happening man?'

'Good question.'

'Remember being here, a second ago?'

'No.'

'Know how a ROM personality matrix works?'

'Sure, bro, it's a firmware construct.'

...

'Okay, Dix. You *are* a ROM construct. Got me?'

'If you say so,' said the construct. 'Who are you?'

(Gibson, *Neuromancer* (1984): 99)

This is only a metaphorical person, a series of computer algorithms that can mimic the particular speech habits of the dead individual: 'what's happening man?' 'who the fuck are you?' But it cannot achieve any sense of self-identity, because it isn't 'real'. This makes Dix totally predictable, which is one key difference between himself and 'real' people. Wintermute says later, 'you guys...you're a pain. The Flatline here, if you were all like him, it would be real simple. He's a construct, just a bunch of ROM, so he always does what I expect him to. My projections said there wasn't much chance of Molly wandering in on Ashpool's big exit scene, give you one example' (p. 245).

But one of the things that happens as the book proceeds is a sense of Gibson fleshing out the famous experiment devised by Alan Turing, the pioneer of computing practice and theory in the 1940s and 1950s, to test whether a machine can ever achieve 'consciousness'. The Turing Test postulates a closed space, in which there might be a human being or a computer. Turing wondered how many questions it would take a human experimenter before he or she could determine who or what was in this box. In the early days of computing it was relatively easy to detect a computer's responses; as computing becomes increasingly sophisticated, so it gets harder. In Gibson's novel, Dix is a dramatisation of the Turing Test. He seems to do everything a consciousness does; and by this I mean more than that he answers back, and laughs, and thinks: I mean that he desires in a way a machine cannot desire – he desires to die. 'Hey asshole,' he says to Wintermute, '...what about me? what about my payoff?' Case asks him what his payoff from Wintermute is to be. 'I want to be erased,' the construct said. 'I told you that, remember?' (p. 246). Dix is 'bothered' by his limbo status; the construct is self-aware and unhappy with its self-awareness:

> 'How you doing, Dixie?'
>   'I'm dead, Case...'
>   'How's it feel?'
>   'It doesn't.'
>   'Bother you?'
>   'What bothers me is, nothin' does.'
>
> (Gibson, *Neuromancer* (1984): 130)

Dix is only one of the characters who are presented to us as a way of problematising our accepted, traditional notions of character. Armitage, unlike Dix, appears to be flesh-and-blood, as real as any human being. But, as the novel progresses, the other characters start to have their doubts: 'that guy, doesn't have any life going, in private…Sits and stares at the wall man' (p. 117). We slowly realise that 'Armitage' is a sort of flesh construct, a ROM personality built around the recovered fragments of a 'real' personality called Corto, who was nearly killed on the 'Screaming Fist' military raid. Corto eventually breaks through Armitage, but Corto is insane where Armitage was rational; Corto sets off and kills himself where Armitage displayed habits of self-preservation. In other words, Corto is less 'real' a character than the artificial 'Armitage'. The novel is full of 'real' characters who act like zombies, like the prostitutes in the Freeside brothel who operate with a neural cut-out so that they don't have to experience the things they do. On the other hand, one of the most vivid 'characters' in the novel is Wintermute himself, who is not 'real', at least until the end. The net effect of all this is to create a situation where 'real' and 'construct' start to blur. Immediately after Wintermute complains to Case that constructs like Dix are predictable and human beings not, Case asks why the old man Ashpool committed suicide. Wintermute's reply starts with a standard disavowal that he doesn't know because humans are simply unpredictable; but he goes on to admit not only that he knows the reason for the suicide, but that he prompted it, in an indirect way. In other words, Ashpool was as 'predictable' as any AI:

> 'Why does anybody kill himself?' The figure shrugged. 'I guess I know, if anybody does, but it would take me twelve hours to explain the various factors in his history and how they interrelate…3Jane figured a way to fiddle the program that controlled his cryogenic system…so basically *she* killed him…Well, actually, I guess I did give 3Jane the odd hint…
>
> (Gibson, *Neuromancer* (1984): 245)

Wintermute frequently comes over in this novel as – a significant pun – virtually omniscient, god-like. This could be an instance of the SF text that plays with secular versions of religious notions; a novel without a God that invents one, a computer one, as it goes on. Or perhaps we should follow the French girl's analysis and think in terms less of God and more of Demons. At one point inside Wintermute, Case gets to the root of the issue of identity that I have been interrogating here, the suggestion that even our own 'identity', that sense of ourselves that we prize so dearly, may only be a 'metaphor' too:

> 'Can you read my mind, Finn?' He grimaced. 'Wintermute, I mean.'
>
> 'Minds aren't *read*. See, you've still got the paradigms print gave you, and you're barely print-literate. I can *access* your memory, but that's not the same as your mind.'
>
> (Gibson, *Neuromancer* (1984): 204)

Case and Wintermute are here trading different metaphors of consciousness. Case falls back on the idea that consciousness is like a book, like the book we are reading, perhaps; this is a suitably self-reflexive notion, because, of course, literally, Case's consciousness is like a book, in fact it *is* a book. Wintermute, on the other hand, insists that consciousness is like a computer programme. This debate is essentially a philosophical debate, something *Neuromancer* is full of. For instance, Case, trapped inside Wintermute's cyberspace imitation of reality, is curious as to whether the computer simulation continues out of the window to include things he can't see. Wintermute refers to the famous philosophical question associated with English eighteenth-century thinker George Berkeley, who wondered whether a tree that falls in the forest where nobody sees it makes a sound. Case looks out the virtual window and asks, 'what's out there? New York? Or does it just stop?' 'Well,' Wintermute replies, 'it's like that tree, you know? Falls in the woods, but maybe there's nobody to hear it' (p. 203). This novel inhabits the philosophical space that argues over the question of 'consciousness'; something philosophers have been arguing over for thousands of years.

Samuel Delany, writing about *Neuromancer*, also sees in the cyborg a fascination with the process of metaphor, in this novel and in the genre we call 'cyberpunk' as a whole. In an essay about Donna Harraway's 'Manifesto for Cyborgs' he identifies a *surplus* of metaphor in the notion of the cyborg:

> A metaphor (or simile) always produces a logical structure – a structure that, in itself, is almost always wholly semantic. (Why is a raven like a writing desk? Because Poe wrote on both.) But there's always a psychological surplus, poetic and organised far more at the level of the letter. (Feathers, leather, wings, wood, stone, bone, beak, brass, eyes, handles, claws, drawers...) and the tension between the logical semantic structure and the psychological, poetic surplus is, I think, what produces the energy and vividness of metaphor.
>
> (Delany 1994: 174)

Delany's insight is that, although a metaphor is used to a particular end, to make a specific point or anchor a specific allusion, it tends to carry with itself a wider range of suggestion than is strictly relevant. If somebody says 'I wouldn't touch that with a bargepole', we understand that this person does not want to get involved with the matter in question, but we may also imagine an actual person with an actual bargepole, perhaps pushing a barge away from collision with a riverbank, even though this image is not strictly relevant to the point being made. It is this metaphorical surplus, that Delany calls 'poetic', that provides the tremendous and intricate detail for Gibson's vision; it is all generated out of the central metaphors of cyberspace, consciousness/ identity and the social system as a metaphorical organism. In so far as all the detail proceeds from this carefully wrought structure, *Neuromancer* is a wonderfully tightly controlled work of art.

The symbolic novum of the novel reflects lucidly back on our experience of living in the world, whilst allowing the startling and poetic encounter with otherness that is the strength of the science-fictional mode. Scott Bukatman thinks that cyberpunk 'remains the most sustained manifestation' of what he calls 'terminal identity', the computer-mediated end of old models of subjectivity, in contemporary culture; and he regards Gibson as 'indisputably the finest of the cyberpunk writers' because 'he is the most poetic, and the most physical – the most erotic...in the climactic cyberspatial transcendence at the end of *Neuromancer*, Case's mouth fills with "the aching taste of blue" – perhaps the taste of the machine, the taste of technology' (Bukatman 1993: 328–9). Science fiction is still the best way to experience that distinctive, strange and impossible taste.

6

CONCLUSION

This study has argued for science fiction as a symbolist genre, one distinguished from other symbolist modes of literature by the fact that its symbols are deployed within a rationalised and materialist discourse, most usually that of 'science' and 'pseudo-science'. The point of this symbolic medium is to connect the exploration of the encounter with difference to our experience of being-in-the-world. Gwyneth Jones argues that 'what is needed' with SF 'is not a suspension of disbelief, it is an active process of translation'.

> This is not necessarily a profound or sophisticated intellectual exercise. There is very little enlightenment to be gained in consciously recognising the starship Enterprise, in the original series, as a US navy nuclear submarine cruising aimlessly around the Pacific, dispensing the morality of the Age of Liberalism at a vaguely doveish period in the Cold War. But there is nothing like constructing a world, or recognising a constructed world, for teaching you to see your own world as a construct. It is the existence of the technique that is significant.
>
> (Jones 1999: 6)

Jones is by no means alone in seeing positive good in SF because of its ability to open the minds of its readers to ways of seeing that challenge the conventional, the narrow minded or the bigoted. Jones's example, the TV series *Star Trek*, is well chosen, in that SF works best in the sort of thoroughly popular and populist idiom that TV represents. SF is able vigorously to popularise relativisms that challenge the monolithic and oppressive ideologies of much human culture. Jones has her own utopian vision, that in this twenty-first century 'through SF-inflected "literature" the relativism of both Einstein and Saussure will percolate slowly, slowly into the popular consciousness', Jones's references to Albert Einstein (1879–1955) and Ferdinand de Saussure (1857–1913) invoke usefully iconic figures. Einstein is remembered today for his Theory of Relativity, with its insight that space, time, mass and velocity are all interrelated quantities that can never be measured in absolute terms but only relative to one another. Saussure developed a theory of linguistics which sees language as a system of signs, whose elements are only comprehensible in relation to one another. These two perspectives on relativism, that of the scientist and that of the semanticist, of the different discourses of scientific relativism and of the arbitrariness of the signifier, come together in rational, structural fabulation, or 'science fiction'. SF now has the job of providing for us the symbols with which conceptualisation of our rapidly changing world is even possible. As John Clute says:

> No longer has information any tangible, kinetic analogue in the world of the senses, or in the imaginations of writers of fiction. Gone are the great arrays of vacuum tubes, the thousands of toggles that heroes of space fiction would flick *almost* faster than the eye could see as they dodged space 'torpedoes', outflanked alien 'battle lines', steered through asteroid 'storms'; gone, more importantly, is any sustained sense of the autonomy, in space and time, of gross visible individual

human actions. And if 'actions' are now invisible, then our fates are likewise beyond our grasp. We no longer feel that we penetrate the future; futures penetrate us.

(Clute, quoted in Bukatman 1993: 1–2)

Cyberpunk is only one of the many versions of SF that finds ways of expressing, of materialising, this complex situation; and the backwards trajectory of a future that is piercing through our present into our past precisely maps out the dialectic of nostalgia and prediction that defines what SF is.

The SF obsession with alien encounter, which has spilled out into culture in general in the last decade or so, is the key trope. Science fiction is about the encounter with difference. At its best, science fiction provides the most supple and the most popular means of exploring questions of diversity and difference; it opens up new possibilities; it makes us *think*. Science fiction most effectively addresses the questions that have defined the age we live in: technology, gender, race, history. As a literature of ideas, where the emphasis is less on literary technique, SF has been able to trade in the concepts of philosophy, theory, history and politics in vivid and popular ways. More than this, there is a fundamental vigour and energy to SF fabulation that is invigorating and energising for the readers or viewers. Science fiction is the dominant mode of imaginative writing today, a body of work that encourages readers to take nothing for granted, to challenge all their assumptions, to think through how things might be different. It is time and again, accordingly, a revolutionary mode of writing.

Alterity, the radical alterity of human diversity, is something we need to train ourselves into accepting. The alternative is, one way or another, conceptually to squeeze everybody else into a caricature version of ourselves. Nor is it enough merely to 'be aware' of alterity, because that too is a form of dismissal. Thomas Docherty's *Alterities*, a complex study of postmodern culture, politics and ethics, sees what he unabashedly calls 'love' as the crucial ingredient, and this 'love' requires the active apprehension of difference: 'there has to be the *encounter* with alterity; and it is such an encounter which is constitutive of a stronger – philosophical – version of love' (Docherty 1996: 206–7). The passion which SF fans feel for their favourite books, films and comics, this love is precisely this.

GLOSSARY

AI Abbreviation for 'Artificial Intelligence', an as-yet uninvented computer program of such sophistication and complexity that it has the same qualities as human consciousness. To date, computers are no more than the sum of their programs, but some thinkers argue that eventually a computer will become sentient, able to think in ways that supersede their programs and which their programmers could not anticipate. The British computing pioneer and philosopher Alan Turing (1912–54) devised a test to determine whether a computer has achieved AI [see **Turing Test**].

Allegory A metaphorical narrative or description, in which all the characters and events of the tale both function on their own terms and also refer figuratively to a hidden network of meaning. An example is John Bunyan's novel *The Pilgrim's Progress* (1678), where a character called Christian travels through a landscape away from the City of Destruction and towards the Celestial City. Bunyan's novel is an elaborately worked-through figurative version of the individual Christian's spiritual journey out of sin and towards redemption, in which every character and every event refers allegorically to this scheme. Allegory differs from **symbolism** in that every element in an allegory relates to the figurative pattern.

Alterity The word means 'Otherness', and connects with a body of criticism that is interested in the way literature and culture represent 'the Other'. Categorising a person or group as 'Other' is often a way of excluding them from a definition of normality: for instance, if women are defined as 'other', the

definition dismisses female experience and sets up male experience as the norm. Thomas Docherty's book *Alterities* (1996)
argues that, in order to be fully human, we need actively to seek
out and encounter Alterity, rather than dismissing it in this way.

Cognitive Estrangement Darko Suvin's definition of science
fiction sees the genre as combining 'cognition' – rational or scientific elements – with 'estrangement' – a literary term sometimes
translated as 'alienation', which refers to those aspects of a literary
work that 'estrange' from the familiar and everyday (see p. 7).

Commodity Fetishisation A term from Marxist theory, which
refers to the tendency in a capitalist system (such as prevails in
the Western world today) to imbue 'commodities', objects that
are bought and sold, with a superstitious near-magical quality.
For example, some people desire consumer goods like CD-players
or designer clothes as if they had some kind of magical intrinsic
value; people will spend a lot of money on designer clothes even
though non-designer clothes are just as good at covering them up
and cost a lot less, because they believe there is something intrin-
sically 'special' about the designer label. The term has been taken
up by some critics of science fiction to talk about the way SF, and
SF TV and cinema in particular, is so enamoured of technological
objects, props and fittings, with things like spaceships and ray-
guns.

Cyberpunk A branch of science fiction particularly associated
with the 1980s; the name derives from 'cyber-', a prefix that con-
notes technological systems, and 'punk', the pop music movement of the late 1970s characterised by aggressive
anti-Establishment posturings and a particular youth style.
Following on from novels like William Gibson's *Neuromancer*
(1984) or films such as Ridley Scott's *Blade Runner* (1982), a great
many 'cyberpunk' works were produced. They tend to be focused

on crime storylines, to portray the future as a dirty, grim and exhausting urban jungle, and to be populated with hard-boiled, streetwise characters.

Cyberspace   The prefix 'cyber-' derived originally from 'cybernetics', the study of systems and machines; now it signifies 'machine- or technology-related or dominated'. Cyberspace is the notional space of the internet and virtual reality, a computer-generated environment into which human beings can enter through a computer or a virtual-reality suit. In reality this 'space' is fairly limited, but many science-fiction texts posit a time when cyberspace is an exciting and dynamic realm of possibilities.

Dialectics   The word 'dialectics' derives from the Greek word for argument or debate, and refers to a particular method of doing philosophy by stating a proposition (a *thesis*), then examining its contrary or opposite to see whether it has anything valid to contribute to the debate (the *antithesis*), and finally arriving at a third proposition that incorporates both sides (the *synthesis*). For example: *Thesis*: 'All grown men have beards'. *Antithesis*: 'On the contrary, there some grown men who scrape off their beards and have bald chins'. *Synthesis*: 'All grown men who do not shave have beards'. The word was originally associated with the Greek philosophers Socrates and Plato, whose philosophical works take the form of dialogues between various peoples in which arguments are developed dialectically. The philosopher Fredric Jameson has called dialectics 'stereoscopic thinking', the ability to encounter and think through both sides of any argument.

Discourse   In linguistics 'discourse' is the actual practice of people speaking to one another, such that 'discourse analysis' will take examples of 'discourse', for instance a conversation between two people, and analyse it. In criticism more generally, 'discourse' is a term popularised by the French historian and philosopher

Michel Foucault, who takes it to refer to a more general system governed by certain rules that determine what can and cannot be said. Foucault believes these large systems of possible statements are connected to the historical circumstances of a particular culture, so that (for instance) a particular discourse of medicine in nineteenth-century France governs what can and cannot be said about illness and health.

Epistemology is that branch of philosophy concerned with questions of knowledge and knowing (*episteme* is the Greek for knowledge); it asks such questions as 'what can we know?', 'how do we know?' and analyses the processes by which we find things out. It is sometimes contrasted with ontology, that branch of philosophy concerned with questions of being and essence. Some critics have seen a form of popular culture like the detective novel as epistemological (concerned with finding something out – the identity of a murderer, say), where science fiction is sometimes seen as more ontological (concerned with the essence or nature of, for instance, an alien).

Golden Age A term within science-fiction studies used to refer to the period 1938–46 in American SF, a time dominated by the magazine publication of short stories and novels. This was the period when some of the major writers in the genre, particularly Isaac Asimov, Robert Heinlein and A E Van Vogt, were producing some of their best work, and many SF fans look back with nostalgia to this period. Golden Age SF tends to be positive about the possibilities of technological advance, kinetic, full of adventure and romantic.

Gothic Novel Gothic novels were a craze in the late eighteenth and early nineteenth centuries: usually dark tales of horror and the supernatural, frequently set in mysterious castles or amongst wild picturesque landscapes. Some Gothic novels dealt with the terrorising of innocent young women by ghosts, demons or monsters; and the aim of the Gothic mode was to create a sense of terror and awe in the reader that was connected with notions of the **sublime**. Mary Shelley's 1818 Gothic novel *Frankenstein* is seen by many critics as an important early example of science fiction.

Ideology For Karl Marx, ideology was 'false consciousness', a set of beliefs that obscured the truth of the economic basis of society and the violent oppression capitalism necessarily entails. Various people believe various things: for instance, that the fact that some people are rich and some people poor is 'natural and inevitable'; or that 'everybody is equal under the law'; or that 'black people are inferior'. The purpose of these beliefs, according to Marx, is to obscure the truth. Such people, believing these things, are not going to challenge or even recognise the inequalities of wealth in society, and so are not going to want to change them. Subsequent Marxist thinkers have refined Marx's original simple conception of 'ideology' to refer to the system of ideas by which people structure their experience of living in the world; this in turn is not something straightforwardly 'right' or 'wrong', but rather a complex network of various relations and attitudes. Whether we think of ourselves as family members (daughters, sisters and so on), as 'citizens', as 'workers' (which is to say, whether it is our job that most importantly defines who we are for ourselves), as 'students', as 'music-lovers' or 'sportswomen' or whatever – in all these cases and in any others we could name, these categories (family, work, leisure) have already been defined by ideology in a complex relationship with the economic dynamics of late capitalism.

Intertextuality Relationships between two or more texts, characterised by quotation, allusion and other reference. Some critics see all literary works or **texts** as interpenetrated by various memories and references to other texts. In a mode of writing science fiction, intertextuality can become particularly important, with SF fans and writers bringing detailed knowledge of the canon of previous SF texts to every new text, such that any new SF novel about (say) time travel will exist in an intertextual relationship with the other classic works about time travel, from H G Wells's famous novel *The Time Machine* (1895) onwards.

Materialist/ism In philosophy, 'materialism' is defined in opposition to 'idealism', the belief that, although there is a real world, we only have access to it through our perceptions and consciousness, and so therefore only the ideas in our mind are 'real' in any meaningful sense. Materialist philosophers see the matter of reality as an important grounding for philosophical enquiry, so that 'the real world of material objects' precedes thoughts and concepts.

New Wave A term in science-fiction studies referring to a movement of SF authors in the 1960s and early 1970s. The term originated in non-SF cinema, where some radical and experimental French directors of the 1960s such as Truffaut and Jean-Luc Godard were categorised as part of a *nouvelle vague* or 'new wave' of cinema. Some SF writers, like Michael Moorcock, Thomas Disch and J G Ballard, started writing deliberately experimental science fiction that flouted the established conventions of the genre. New Wave SF was experimental in form and subject, and reflected the 1960s countercultural interests in drugs, altered consciousness and sex and an often modishly downbeat outlook.

Novum Darko Suvin's coinage for the 'new thing' or (plural, 'nova') 'new things' that distinguish the SF tale from a conventional literature. This 'point of difference' might be a material object, like a spaceship, a time-machine or a matter-transportation beam; or it might be something conceptual, such as a new form of gender, or a wholly new way of organising society (see p. 6).

Postmodernism   Variously defined and difficult to summarise briefly, 'postmodernity' is seen by some critics as the condition of contemporary culture and society, and 'postmodernism' as the cultural logic that underlies this. Distinguished, as the name suggests, from Modernism (the literary movement dominant at the start of the twentieth century), postmodernism is characterised by certain features of form and style – a mixing-up of different styles and registers, a preference for surface over depth and style over substance, a flattening of emotional depth, incessant quoting and allusion to the point where quotation loses its point, irony, the eruption of popular cultural models into culture as a whole, and a focus on spaces in place of the Modernist fascination with time. A film like *Blade Runner* is sometimes cited as an example of a postmodern text, because it mixes up 'science fiction', 'film noir' and 'action film' styles in a seamless fashion, it is both futuristic and old-fashioned in its styling, it uses 'space' and particularly the disorienting spaces of the city as an organising principle, and because its sophisticated surface gloss and sheer style are more significant than story, character or 'meaning'. I should add that there are theorists of the postmodern who would disagree with pretty much everything I have included in this definition.

Pulps   The 'Pulps' or 'Pulp Magazines' dominated the SF market from the start of the twentieth century through to about the late 1930s. They were printed on cheap paper made from woodpulp, and published disposable adventure stories by hack authors aimed at a popular market. The lack of literary pretension meant that the Pulps were largely ignored, but although Pulp magazines are a thing of the past the phrase 'Pulp SF' lives on as a shorthand way of referring to the crude energy and vigour of early adventure-based, narrative-driven romantic and heroic science fiction.

Realism As a specific term within criticism, 'Realism' refers to a form of the nineteenth-century novel, practised in particular by authors like Honoré de Balzac and Emile Zola, which aimed to reproduce the experience of actually living in the real world with a near-documentary attention to actual fact and attempts to capture a sense of **verisimilitude**. In looser terms, the 'realist' novel is sometimes opposed to the 'fantasy' or 'science-fiction' text, in that 'realism' involves a world that is basically the same as the world we all live in, where SF creates a world that differs in one or more important ways from the real world. In fact, many SF novels use 'realist' techniques, techniques like the accumulation of precisely delineated detail, sociological observation, characters accurately imitated from real life, and an avoidance of poeticism, melodrama, exaggeration and other non-realist techniques.

Self-reflexive A text – a work or film – is said to be 'self-reflexive' when it makes reference to itself in some way, either playfully or else as a deliberate strategy of 'alienation effect', in order to remind the reader or viewer that they are not observing real life.

Simulacrum A 'simulacrum' (plural: 'simulacra') is a copy of some original. The term has currency in contemporary criticism thanks to the work of French philosopher Jean Baudrillard, who has argued that one of the features of the present-day 'postmodern' world is that copies no longer refer to any original, but actually precede the original. So, for instance, for many people TV, having precedence over 'real life', is more real than reality, even though TV started out copying real life. This 'precession of the simulacrum' is called 'hyperreality' by Baudrillard.

Sublime, the The eighteenth-century thinker Edmund Burke distinguished between 'the beautiful' and 'the sublime'. Beauty, he argued, was to be found in harmony, delicacy and smoothness, and provided small-scale aesthetic pleasure. The sublime, on the other hand, was on a much larger scale, was magnificent and produced feelings of awe and even terror. Burke argued that lakes, hills, day and women might be beautiful, but the ocean, mountains, night and men were sublime. **Gothic Novels** in part aimed to produce the sensations of awe and terror by dwelling on awe-inspiring and terrifying scenery and events. science fiction, deriving from Gothic, has carried through this project: many SF texts aim to reproduce the sense of awe and wonder of the sublime by including enormous machines or massive galactic and stellar environments.

Symbolism A symbol is a figurative device that refers to something other than its straightforward connotations, and is linked to metaphor and **allegory**: so a 'rose' is a flower, but is also frequently used as a symbol for a number of things with (for instance) pastoral, patriotic or political connotations. Symbolism differs from allegory in that, where allegory refers to a single specific scheme of meaning, a symbol can mean different things to different people. 'Symbolism' as a literary movement flourished in Europe towards the end of the nineteenth century, in which poets such as Mallarmé and Rimbaud evoked symbols to create subtle and allusive effects.

Text Partly a term that includes a variety of examples of cultural production, books, plays, poems, films, TV shows, pop songs, and even (according to some) paintings, clothes – anything, in short, that can be 'read' as existing within a certain network of signification. A 'text' is a more general term than 'book' or 'film'. It is also sometimes distinguished from 'work', which has the implication of something 'worked' or created by an artist or artisan. 'Text' is more open, less focused on the author, and suggests something still in the process of being 'written' by the processes of critical and readerly or viewerly interpretation and re-interpretation.

Trope A figure of speech or particular strategy in using language. We might say that the phrase 'I feel trapped and tongue-tied' utilises the tropes of imprisonment and bondage, or that *2001: A Space Odyssey* uses the trope of a journey or odyssey as a metaphor for human life.

Turing Test Alan Turing devised this test as a thought experiment in 1950. Imagine two closed rooms, one of which contains a person and the other a computer. You cannot enter the rooms, but you can communicate with who or what is inside by typing questions into a terminal and receiving replies. How many questions would it take before you were able to tell which room contained the person and which the machine? In the early days of computing the answers you might receive from the computer would have been obviously repetitive, artificial or consisting of non-sequiturs, but with more modern computing software it takes longer and longer to say which is which. Turing argued that if the tester cannot tell the machine replies apart from the human ones, then the machine has achieved a consciousness that is on a par with human sentience.

Ur-text The prefix 'ur-' is German and means 'primitive, original, earliest appearing'; and an 'ur-text' is the first or earliest appearance of a given text. We might say that the 1977 print of *Star Wars* is the ur-text, the later special edition reissues being subsequent versions of the text.

Verisimilitude Accuracy or closeness to reality. A documentary film might be said to have more 'verisimilitude' than a ballet or an opera.

SELECT BIBLIOGRAPHY

TEXTS

Books

Asimov, Isaac [1942; as novel 1951] (1981) *Foundation*, London: Panther.
—— [1954] (1985) *Caves of Steel*, London: Voyager.
—— [1982] (1984) *Foundation's Edge*, London: Voyager.
Banks, Iain M (1990) *Use of Weapons*, London: Orbit.
Baxter, Stephen (1998) *Titan*, London: Voyager.
Bradley, Marion Zimmer [1965] (1994) *Star of Danger*, New York: Daw.
—— (1978) *Stormqueen*, Bristol: Severn House.
—— [1985] (1993) *The Best of Marion Zimmer Bradley*, ed. Martin H Greenberg, London: Orbit.
Burroughs, Edgar Rice [1912] (1973) *A Princess of Mars*, New York: Del Rey Books.
Butler, Octavia E [1979] (1988) *Kindred*, London: Women's Press.
—— [1987] (1997) *Dawn*, New York: Warner Books.
—— [1988] (1997) *Adulthood Rites*, New York: Warner Books.
Cherryh, C J [1982] (1989) *Port Eternity*, London, VGSF.
Delany, Samuel [1968] (1970) *The Einstein Intersection*, London: Sphere Books.
Dick, Philip K [1969] (1988) *Ubik*, London: Grafton.
—— [1972] (1984) *Do Androids Dream of Electric Sheep?*, London: Grafton.
Gibson, William [1984] (1993) *Neuromancer*, London: HarperCollins.
Heinlein, Robert [1959] (1998) *Starship Troopers*, London, New English Library.
—— [1961] (1993) *Stranger in a Strange Land*, London: New English Library.
—— [1964] (1976) *Farnham's Freehold*, London: New English Library.
Herbert, Frank [1965] (1989) *Dune*, London: New English Library.
—— [1967] (1989) *Dune Messiah*, London: New English Library.
Jones, Gwyneth [1991] (1992) *White Queen*, London: Victor Gollancz.
Kessel, John (1995) *Good News From Outer Space*, London: Orb Books.

Le Guin, Ursula [1969] (1991) *The Left Hand of Darkness*, London: Futura.

Lem, Stanislaw [1961; 1971; 1975] (1981) *Solaris; A Perfect Vacuum; The Chain of Chance*, trans. Joanna Kilmartin, Steve Cox, Louis Iribarne and Michael Kandel, Harmondsworth: Penguin.

McAuley, Paul (1997) *Child of the River: the First Book of Confluence*, London: Victor Gollancz.

—— (1998) *Ancients of Days: the Second Book of Confluence*, London: Orion.

—— (1999) *Shrine of Stars: the Third Book of Confluence*, London: Orion.

McCaffrey, Anne [1969] (1998) *The Ship Who Sang*, London: Corgi.

Meaney, John (1998) *To Hold Infinity*, London: Bantam.

Milton, John [1674] (1993) *Paradise Lost*, ed. Scott Elledge, New York: Norton.

Moorcock, Michael (1974) *The Land Leviathan*, London: Mayflower .

—— (1993) *The Cornelius Quartet*, London: Victor Gollancz.

Robinson, Kim Stanley [1992] (1996) *Red Mars*, London: Voyager.

Russ, Joanna (1972) 'When It Changed', in *Again, Dangerous Visions*, ed. Harlan Ellison, New York: Doubleday.

—— [1975] (1985) *The Female Man*, London: Women's Press.

Shelley, Mary [1818] (1992) *Frankenstein, or the Modern Prometheus*, ed. Maurice Hindle, Harmondsworth: Penguin.

Smith, E E 'Doc' [1934] (1997) *Triplanetary*, Epsom: Ripping Publications.

Tepper, Sheri [1981] (1996) *Grass*, London: HarperCollins.

Tiptree, James Jr [1973; in book form 1975] (1979) 'The Women Men Don't See', in *Warm Worlds and Otherwise*, New York: Del Rey Books.

Watson, Ian (1975) *The Jonah Kit*, London: VGSF.

Wells, H G [1895–1901] (1995) *The Time Machine, The Island of Doctor Moreau, The War of the Worlds, The First Men in the Moon*, in *The Science Fiction, Volume 1*, London: Phoenix.

Film and TV

Alien (1979: dir. Ridley Scott)

Aliens (1986: dir. James Cameron)

Alien 3 (1992: dir. David Fincher)

Alien Resurrection (1997: dir. Jean-Pierre Jeunet)

Apollo 13 (1996: dir. Ron Howard)

Blade Runner (1982: dir. Ridley Scott)

Lost in Space (1998: dir. Stephen Hopkins)

Men in Black (1997: dir. Barry Sonnenfeld)
Predator (1987: dir. John McTiernan)
Robocop (1987, dir. Paul Verhoeven)
Star Trek (TV episode: 'Let That Be Your Last Battlefield')
Star Trek: the Next Generation (TV episodes: 'The Best of Both Worlds I
        and II'; 'The Masterpiece Society'; 'Darmok at Jilad')
Star Trek 2: the Wrath of Khan (1982, dir. Nicholas Meyer)
Star Trek 3: the Search for Spock (1984, dir. Leonard Nimoy)
Star Trek 4: the Voyage Home (1986, dir. Leonard Nimoy)
Star Wars (1977: dir. George Lucas)
Star Wars: the Empire Strikes Back (1980: dir. Irvin Kerschner)
Star Wars: Return of the Jedi (1983: dir. Richard Marquand)
Star Wars: The Phantom Menace (1999: dir. George Lucas)
Westworld (1973: dir. Michael Crichton)
2001: A Space Odyssey (1968: dir. Stanley Kubrick)

CRITICISM

Abrams, M H (1985) *A Glossary of Literary Terms*, 5th edition, Fort Worth,
    TX: Holt, Rinehart and Winston.

Aldiss, Brian [1973] (1986) *Billion Year Spree: the History of Science
    Fiction*, London: Wiedenfeld and Nicolson. Updated as *Trillion Year
    Spree*, London: Gollancz.

Armitt, Lucie (ed.) (1991) *Where No Man Has Gone Before: Women and
    Science Fiction*, London and New York: Routledge

Barr, Marleen S (1987) *Alien To Femininity: Speculative Fiction and
    Feminist Theory*, Westport, CT: Greenwood Press.

—— (1993) *Lost in Space: Probing Feminist Science Fiction and Beyond*,
    Chapel Hill: University of North Carolina Press.

Barron, Neil (ed.) (1995) *Anatomy of Wonder: A Critical Guide to Science
    Fiction*, 4th edition, New York: Bowker.

Broderick, Damien (1995) *Reading by Starlight: Postmodern Science
    Fiction*, London and New York: Routledge.

Bukatman, Scott (1993) *Terminal Identity: the Virtual Subject in
    Postmodern Science Fiction*, Durham, NC and London: Duke
    University Press.

Clute, John (1995) *Look at the Evidence: Essays and Reviews*, Liverpool:
    Liverpool University Press.

Clute, John and Peter Nicholls (eds) (1993) *The Encyclopedia of Science Fiction*, London: Orbit.

Consalio, Mia (1996) *Discourses of Race in Science Fiction*, New York: Newsday.

Csicsery-Ronay Jr, Istvan (1991) 'Science Fiction and Postmodernism', *Science-Fiction Studies* 18:3, 305–8.

Delany, Samuel (1994) *Silent Interviews. On Language, Race, Sex, Science Fiction and Some Comics*, Hanover, PA and London: Wesleyan University Press.

Dery, Mark (ed.) (1993) 'Flame Wars: the Discourse of Cyberculture' *The South Atlantic Quarterly* 92:4, Fall.

Docherty, Thomas (1996) *Alterities: Criticism, History, Representation*, Oxford: Clarendon Press.

Donawerth, Jane (1997) *Frankenstein's Daughters: Women Writing Science Fiction*, New York: Syracuse University Press.

Donawerth, Jane and Carol A Kolmerten (eds) (1994) *Utopian and Science Fiction by Women: Worlds of Difference*, Liverpool: Liverpool University Press.

Eshun, Kodwo (1998) *More Brilliant Than the Sun: Adventures in Sonic Fiction*, London: Quartet.

Fredericks, Casey (1982) *The Future of Eternity: Mythologies of Science Fiction and Fantasy*, Bloomington: Indiana University Press.

Freedman, Philip (1984) 'Towards a Theory of Paranoia: the Science Fiction of Philip K Dick', *Science-Fiction Studies* 11:2, 15–24.

Gray, Chris Hables, Heidi J Figuroa-Sarriera and Steven Mentor (eds) (1995) *The Cyborg Handbook*, London: Routledge.

Griffiths, John (1980) *Three Tomorrows: American, British and Soviet Science Fiction*, London: Macmillan.

Harraway, Donna J (1991) 'A Cyborg Manifesto: Science, Technology, and Social-Feminism in the Late Twentieth Century', in *Simians, Cyborgs and Women: The Reinvention of Nature*, London: Free Association Books.

Harrison, Taylor (1996) 'Weaving the Cyborg Shroud: Mourning and Deferral in *Star Trek: the Next Generation*', in Harrison, Projanski, Ono and Helford (eds), *Enterprise Zones: Critical Positions on Star Trek*, Boulder, CO: Westview.

Harvey, John (1995) *Men in Black*, London: Reaktion Books.

Huntington, John (1989) *Rationalising Genius: Ideological Strategies in the Classic American Science Fiction Short Story*, New Brunswick, NJ and London: Rutgers University Press.

James, Edward (1994) *Science Fiction in the 20th Century*, Oxford: Oxford University Press.

Jameson, Frederic (1984) 'Postmodernism, or the Cultural Logic of Late Capitalism', *New Left Review* 143, 53–94.

—— (1990) *Postmodernism, or the Cultural Logic of Late Capitalism*, London: Verso.

Jenkins, Henry (1992) *Textual Poachers: Television, Fans and Participatory Culture*, London: Routledge.

Jones, Gwyneth (1999) *Deconstructing the Starships: Science, Fiction and Reality*, Liverpool: Liverpool University Press.

Kristeva, Julia (1982) *Powers of Horror: an Essay in Abjection*, New York: Columbia University Press.

Kuhn, Annette (ed.) (1990) *Alien Zone: Cultural Theory and Contemporary Science Fiction Cinema*, London: Verso.

Lefanu, Sarah (1988) *In the Chinks of the World Machine: Feminism and Science Fiction*, London: Women's Press.

Le Guin, Ursula (1989) *The Language of the Night: Essays on Fantasy and Science Fiction*, London: Women's Press.

Luckhurst, Roger (1997) *'The Angle Between Two Walls': The Fiction of J. G. Ballard*, Liverpool: Liverpool University Press.

—— (1998) 'The Science Fictionalisation of Trauma: Remarks on Narratives of Alien Abduction', *Science-Fiction Studies* 25:1, 1–12.

McCracken, Scott (1998) *Pulp: Reading Popular Fiction*, Manchester: Manchester University Press.

Manlove, Colin Nicholas (1986) *Science Fiction: Ten Explorations*, Kent, OH: Kent State University Press.

Marx, Karl [1867](1976) *Capital*, Vol. 1 (transl. B Foukes), Harmondsworth: Penguin.

Morgan, Chris (1980) *The Shape of Futures Past: the Story of Prediction*, Exeter: Webb and Bower.

Nicholls, Peter (ed.) (1981) *The Encyclopedia of Science Fiction*, London: Granada.

O'Reilly, Timothy (1981) *Frank Herbert*, New York: Ungar.

Parkin, Lance (1999) Letter to *Interzone* 139 (January), 4–5.

Parrinder, Patrick (ed.) (1979) *Science Fiction: A Critical Guide*, London: Longman.

—— (1980) *Science Fiction: its Criticism and Teaching*, London and New York: Methuen.

Roberts, Robin (1993) *A New Species: Gender and Science in Science Fiction*, Urbana: University of Illinois Press.

Russ, Joanna (1972) 'The Image of Women in Science Fiction', in S K Cornillon (ed.) *Images of Women in Fiction*, Bowling Green, KY: Bowling Green University Popular Press.

Scholes, Robert (1975) *Structural Fabulation: An Essay on Fiction of the Future*, Bloomington: Indiana University Press.

Slusser, George and Tom Shippey (eds) (1992) *Fiction 2000: Cyberpunk and the Future of Narrative*, Athens and London: University of Georgia Press.

Suvin, Darko (1979) *Metamorphoses of Science Fiction: On the Poetics and History of a Literary Genre*, New Haven, CT: Yale University Press.

Tulloch, John and Henry Jenkins (1995) *Science Fiction Audiences*, London: Routledge.

Westfahl, Gary (1999) 'Janeways and Thaneways; the Better Half, and Worse Half, of Science Fiction Television', *Interzone* 140 (February), 31–3.

Wolmark, Jenny (1994) *Aliens and Others: Science Fiction, Feminism and Postmodernism*, New York and London: Harvester.

INDEX